THE
NATURAL
COOK

MAXIMUM TASTE ZERO WASTE

THE NATURAL COOK

MATT STONE

MURDOCH BOOKS
SYDNEY · LONDON

CONTENTS

INTRODUCTION

Food, nutrition and eating are the most basic elements of life. Eat well and you live well. Cook creatively and life becomes more interesting and enjoyable. Consider the provenance of your food and live a more sustainable life. These themes are central to my philosophy of food and cooking.

The media is awash with information about organic produce, the ethical sourcing of food and the environmental sustainability of farming practices. It can be a bit much to take in. I hope this book helps to cut through the marketing and hype to show that eating healthily and ethically doesn't have to be an enormous burden. Making interesting, creative, healthy meals isn't hard to do. With a little effort and thought it soon becomes second nature.

Where your food comes from is the starting point for good eating. Where was it grown? How far has it travelled? How has it been processed or preserved? How much nutritional value has it lost along the way? Buying fresh local produce, or even growing your own, can reduce your environmental footprint, reduce waste and improve the quality of the food you bring into your kitchen.

I make a lot of things from scratch in this book. This can take a little more effort than buying the same product from the supermarket but the benefits are enormous. You have traceability of your ingredients. You know exactly what you're eating. And, as a bonus, making your own cheese, rolling your own oats or milling your own flour can be lots of fun!

The array of native Australian flavours and ingredients is mind-blowing. Some people say our native herbs and spices are too tannic or astringent to use, but when properly balanced with other flavours in the dish they can be the perfect addition.

A number of my recipes incorporate native ingredients. While they can be difficult to find in your local supermarket, the first step to making them more readily available is to create consumer demand by using them every day, not just every now and then. We need to move forward from the gimmicky 'bush tucker' movement of the past and embrace these amazing ingredients in a natural way.

I'd like to see native herbs and spices become staples in every cook's pantry. I'd like home cooks to have fun with these ingredients, to be creative in the kitchen and not automatically fall back on the traditional condiments and flavours that arrived with European settlement.

Cooks who don't have easy access to Australian fruits, herbs and spices can apply the same philosophy by using local equivalents of native flavours. The aim is to be flexible and creative with what is at hand.

I also take inspiration from proven traditional cooking techniques, and these provide the foundation for many recipes in this book. Fermenting and pickling are trendy at the moment but they've been used for health benefits and preservation for centuries – as have making dairy products, milling flour and rolling oats. I think we need to respect that history and integrate these processes into our kitchens without them being a novelty.

Above all, I hope this book provokes thought. I want people to question their habits in the kitchen and be willing to try something new – whether it's making broth, cooking with quandongs, starting a worm farm, foraging for wild food or making a curry paste using fresh lemon myrtle instead of kaffir lime leaves. I also hope it encourages everyone to ask questions about how their food is made and where it comes from.

Researching the food in your kitchen is never going to be wasted time. The more you understand your food, the healthier, more enjoyable and more satisfying it will be. And that benefits both body and soul.

MY STORY

I got my first job as a kitchen hand at Café Forte soon after my family moved to Margaret River in Western Australia in 2002. I worked at night and surfed in the mornings. It was the ideal life for a surf-crazy teenager.

Strangely, I loved it in the kitchen. Working until midnight, getting soaked washing dishes, getting yelled at, the rush of service. It was at Café Forte that I decided I wanted to be a chef. I constantly asked questions about food and cooking. I learned the basics and my duties grew weekly. My love of food had started.

Next came a job at a large pub in Perth. It sucked. Making sauces from powder and buying everything as pre-made as possible. It confused the hell out of me and I lost my spark for cooking. After about six months, I busted my knee in a Grinspoon moshpit and was out of action for a few months. The plus side was that I never had to work at the pub again.

Back in Margaret River to recuperate, I started looking for a job in a proper restaurant – one that cooked real food. I got a job at Leeuwin Estate winery and its sous chef, Tim Taylor, took me under his wing over two summers and taught me many skills I still use today. Tim and I have remained good mates ever since.

I became hungry for more and wanted to work at the best restaurant I could. Star Anise in Perth was Western Australia's most highly regarded restaurant at the time, so I applied for a job there, met the chef David Coomer and he hired me on the spot. I loved it at Star Anise. I worked my way up through the kitchen and was promoted to sous chef when I was 20 years old. It was a difficult task to learn how to run a kitchen but thankfully David was there to help. He is an amazing self-taught chef with a passion for great produce and the most important mentor in the kitchen I've ever had. Over four years he fine-tuned my skills, pushed me to the limits and made me want to be the best chef I could be.

After Star Anise I had a few jobs around Perth but nothing excited me. Then I was approached about a restaurant by designer, artist, restaurateur, florist and environmentalist Joost Bakker. It would be a restaurant made entirely from recycled or recyclable materials that served wholesome, delicious food. I saw a drawing of the place – it was a cube covered in plants, and incorporated worm farms, growing plants and recycling water. Crazy!

At this stage in my career, all of these things were unknown to me and I said no to the job offer at first – but I quickly came around. I flew to Melbourne to meet Joost and we hit it off immediately. His work is incredible. He uses recycled materials and seasonal flowers and plants to create amazing installations in cafés, bars and restaurants all over town. He has been a great inspiration and helped me develop my philosophy around healthy eating and sustainability. He's also a great mate.

We had fantastic success at the Greenhouse restaurant in Perth, serving great coffee and booze as well as simple, seasonal, healthy and affordable food. We did breakfast, had a takeaway pastry window, an à la carte menu for lunch, and a share menu for dinner. It was a huge undertaking for a 22-year-old and I couldn't have done it without my sous chef Courtney Gibb.

Courtney and I had worked at Star Anise together and he was my first choice as right-hand man. We made a great team. Courtney took care of pastry and I looked after the savoury side of things, although we would collaborate on both menus. As my profile grew, so did Courtney's workload. Soon enough he was running the kitchen and I worked on menu development, trained the apprentices and did the pass for the big services and events to promote the restaurant. Courtney is a legend.

In our first year I was named *Gourmet Traveller* Best Young Chef and Best Young Talent in the *WA Good Food Guide* as well as the Greenhouse being awarded the Guide's Best New Restaurant. Shortly afterwards I appeared on the first-ever episode of (the short-lived) *Iron Chef Australia*, battling against Neil Perry. Of course, I lost, but only by four points. I've also made two seasons of *Recipes that Rock*, a cooking show with Blur bass-player Alex James, and have appeared on *MasterChef Australia* multiple times.

Joost and I have since created pop-up Greenhouse restaurants in Sydney and Melbourne, both in amazing settings. More recently I've worked as head chef at Joost's zero-waste restaurants Silo and Brothl in Melbourne, and at Oakridge Estate in the Yarra Valley, where I've set up a productive garden to supplement a menu built around locally sourced produce.

1.
FRESHLY ROLLED & MILLED

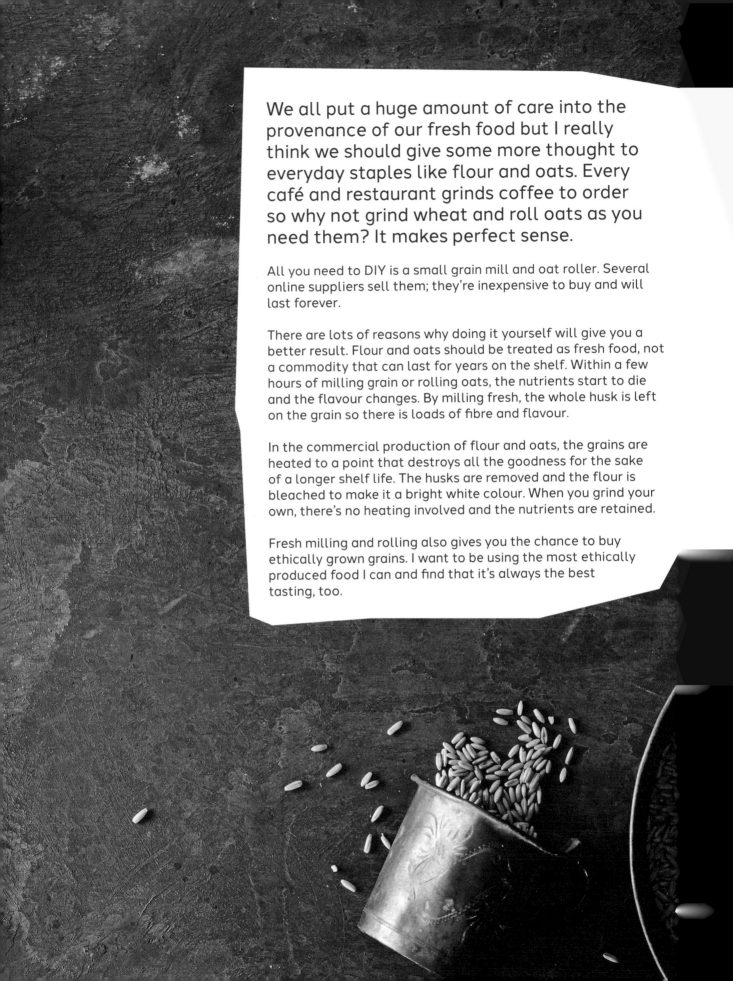

We all put a huge amount of care into the provenance of our fresh food but I really think we should give some more thought to everyday staples like flour and oats. Every café and restaurant grinds coffee to order so why not grind wheat and roll oats as you need them? It makes perfect sense.

All you need to DIY is a small grain mill and oat roller. Several online suppliers sell them; they're inexpensive to buy and will last forever.

There are lots of reasons why doing it yourself will give you a better result. Flour and oats should be treated as fresh food, not a commodity that can last for years on the shelf. Within a few hours of milling grain or rolling oats, the nutrients start to die and the flavour changes. By milling fresh, the whole husk is left on the grain so there is loads of fibre and flavour.

In the commercial production of flour and oats, the grains are heated to a point that destroys all the goodness for the sake of a longer shelf life. The husks are removed and the flour is bleached to make it a bright white colour. When you grind your own, there's no heating involved and the nutrients are retained.

Fresh milling and rolling also gives you the chance to buy ethically grown grains. I want to be using the most ethically produced food I can and find that it's always the best tasting, too.

GREENHOUSE BREAKFAST MUFFINS

We made this muffin from the day we opened the Greenhouse restaurant until the day I left, and the only complaint we ever got was when they'd sold out. I think I've eaten a few hundred for breakfast in my time.

MAKES 4–6

MUFFINS
100 g (3½ oz) mixed nuts
4 eggs
280 g (10 oz) raw (demerara) sugar
200 g (7 oz) carrots, unpeeled and grated
200 g (7 oz) apples, unpeeled and grated
150 ml (5 fl oz) vegetable oil
300 g (10½ oz/2 cups) freshly milled flour
2 teaspoons baking powder
2 teaspoons ground cinnamon
¼ teaspoon salt

TOPPING
50 g (1¾ oz) cold butter
70 g (2½ oz) freshly milled flour
50 g (1¾ oz/½ cup) freshly rolled oats
50 g (1¾ oz) sunflower seeds
1 teaspoon vegetable oil
3 teaspoons honey

NOTE: *Any nuts can be used in this muffin – whatever you have in the pantry, really. I like to use walnuts or hazelnuts. You can replace the carrot with more apple if you like and, on top of that, you can also substitute the apple with pear.*

Dry-toast the nuts in a heavy-based frying pan over medium–high heat for 3–5 minutes until fragrant and golden, then roughly chop. Whisk the eggs together in a large mixing bowl and once things start to get foamy, slowly begin to pour in the sugar. Keep whisking until the sugar has dissolved and the mixture has doubled in size. Whisk in the carrot, apple, oil and toasted nuts. Use a spatula to gently fold in the flour, baking powder, cinnamon and salt.

The mixture can be baked straight away but I suggest leaving it in the fridge overnight. This will give the flour a chance to hydrate and the baking powder to activate, resulting in a more consistent muffin texture. The mix will keep for 3–4 days in the fridge so it's not a bad idea to make a double batch and bake every second day so you can have fresh muffins all week with little fuss.

Preheat the oven to 180°C (350°F). For the topping, place the cold butter and flour in a bowl and rub together with your fingertips. Add the oats, seeds and oil, mix well, then mix in the honey. You want a crumble-type mixture. If it's too dry, add a splash of water to get it to a lovely, crumbly consistency.

Grease a 12-hole standard (60 ml/⅓ cup) muffin tin and line the holes with squares of baking paper. Spoon in the muffin mixture and press it down to the level of the tin.

Cover the top of the muffins with the crumbly topping mixture. Place the tray in the oven and cook for about 25 minutes. Check the muffins at 15 minutes and every 5 minutes from there. The good ol' skewer test is the perfect way to see if they're cooked through (poke a skewer into the middle of a muffin and if it comes out with gloopy mixture attached, keep baking).

Once cooked, remove the muffins from the oven and leave to cool in the tin for 5–10 minutes. Remove them from the tin, peel off the baking paper and place on a wire rack.

They're best eaten the day they're cooked with a nice cup of tea, but will hold for brekkie the next day, too.

GRANOLA

Granola can be bloody expensive when bought at the shops. Stuff that! Making your own is a great way to save money and have control over the quality of the ingredients used. You can grab any nuts you have at the back of the pantry instead of almonds.

SERVES 8–10

100 g (3½ oz) butter
350 g (12 oz/1 cup) honey
3 teaspoons ground cinnamon
1 teaspoon ground cloves
570 g (1 lb 4½ oz/5¾ cups) freshly rolled oats
80 g (2¾ oz/½ cup) almonds, coarsely chopped
1 teaspoon salt

OPTIONAL
160 g (5½ oz) mixed dried fruits, such as apricots, figs and raisins, finely chopped

Preheat the oven to 160°C (320°F).

Put the butter, honey and spices into a small saucepan and bring to a gentle boil, stirring now and then until the butter has completely melted and the ingredients are nicely combined. Meanwhile, place the oats, almonds and salt into a mixing bowl. Pour over the hot honey butter and mix everything together well.

Line a large baking tray with baking paper. Spread a thin layer of the oat mixture over the tray (you might need to use two trays for this). Put the granola in the oven for about 10 minutes until golden. You may need to poke it around a bit, depending on the hot spots in your oven. Once golden, remove from the oven and leave it to cool.

When cool enough to touch, gently break apart the granola with your hands. Once fully cool, add the dried fruit, if using, and store in an airtight container or jar. The granola will keep for up to 2 weeks.

MUESLI BARS

Quick and easy, these muesli bars only require a small amount of weekend prep time, and are the ideal snack when your energy levels are a little low. There is a bit of sugar in this recipe but I'm certain these are healthier and tastier than any muesli bar from a supermarket shelf. You can use any fruit, nuts or seeds in your pantry, or to your taste.

MAKES 6–8

350 g (12 oz) freshly
  rolled oats
80 g (2¾ oz/½ cup) almonds,
  coarsely chopped
55 g (2 oz/⅓ cup)
  sunflower seeds
200 g (7 oz) raw
  (demerara) sugar
150 g (5½ oz) butter
100 g (3½ oz) honey
2 teaspoons salt
2 teaspoons ground
  wattleseed (optional)
75 g (2¾ oz/⅓ cup) dried figs,
  finely chopped
80 g (2¾ oz/½ cup) dried
  apricots, finely chopped
85 g (3 oz/½ cup) raisins

NOTE: *Wattleseed is now available in many supermarkets but can also be found easily online. It imparts a lovely cacao and hazelnut flavour.*

Preheat the oven to 170°C (340°F). Mix the oats, almonds and sunflower seeds together and place on a baking tray lined with baking paper. Roast in the oven for about 10–15 minutes until golden. You may need to give the tray a shake every 5 minutes if your oven temperature isn't even.

Put the sugar, butter, honey, salt and wattleseed, if using, into a medium saucepan over medium heat and bring to the boil. Stir and cook until all the sugar has dissolved. While the oat and butter mixtures are both hot, place them together in a mixing bowl along with the dried fruits and stir well. The mix should be shiny and sticky.

The mix now needs to be pressed into a large rectangular or square tin. Any tin will work, although one with a depth of about 2–3 cm (¾–1¼ inches) is ideal.

Firmly press the mixture into the tin, leaving no gaps. The muesli bars will fall apart when you cut them if the mixture isn't packed firmly enough at this stage.

Place the tin in the fridge for a couple of hours for the muesli mixture to set. Take it out and run a knife around the edges to help release the muesli. Place a chopping board over the tin and flip it over. Tap the tin to set the mixture free.

Cut the bars as big as you like. I'd suggest about 2 cm (¾ inch) by 10 cm (4 inches) for a decent-sized snack. The bars will keep in an airtight container or tin for a week, easy.

MILLING FLOUR

ROLLING OATS

PORRIDGE

When I was a kid my porridge would always come from a packet, but it's honestly so simple to wake up, roll some oats and make it fresh. Porridge with freshly rolled oats and good quality milk will keep your energy levels high all day.

I like to eat porridge with fresh or poached fruit. Fresh stone fruit or banana is brilliant in summer, and in winter I like poached quince or rhubarb. Just use whatever is around you and in season. A mix of toasted seeds and nuts is also good to have on hand to bring different textures, flavours and nutrients to your breakfast.

SERVES 2

625 ml (21½ fl oz/2½ cups) milk
95 g (3¼ oz/1 cup) freshly rolled oats
1 tablespoon butter
honey, to serve

In a medium saucepan, bring the milk to a gentle boil over low heat, add the oats and stir. Continue stirring like you would a risotto – porridge should not be left to its own devices. You want to cook it for 3–5 minutes, until the milk and oats have come together and the porridge has a pouring consistency.

Stir in the butter and a small pinch of salt at the last minute and drizzle with honey. Seize the day (or retire back to bed with the morning paper).

BARBECUE BREAD

I love homemade bread. This is easy to make and great alongside cheese and dips, and anything that comes off the barbecue. You just need to get the dough going a couple of hours before you want to eat the bread. It's golden and crusty on the outside and soft and rich within. If you're not firing up the barbie, it can be cooked in a non-stick frying pan instead.

MAKES 12

1 tablespoon sugar
1 tablespoon dried yeast
4 tablespoons olive oil,
    plus extra for oiling
    tops and frying
4 tablespoons plain yoghurt
    (or see recipe, page 41)
1 kg (2 lb 4 oz/6⅔ cups)
    freshly milled flour, plus
    extra for dusting
1½ tablespoons salt

In a medium mixing bowl, combine the sugar, yeast, oil, yoghurt and 750 ml (26 fl oz/3 cups) of water. Mix well and let it stand for 10 minutes. Mix the flour and the salt together and add to the water mixture. Knead for 10 minutes until the dough begins to have some resistance when stretched. Lightly oil the sides of the bowl and let the dough sit, covered, for 1 hour. After the hour, lift up one side of the dough and fold in half. Do the same to the other edge, folding it into quarters. Cover and let it sit for another 30 minutes.

Turn the dough out onto a lightly floured work surface and dust some more flour on top of it. Divide the dough into 130 g (4½ oz) portions. Roll the dough into balls and let them sit on the floured surface, covered, for 20 minutes. Re-roll the balls and place them onto an oiled tray, leaving enough space for them to double in size. This will take about 40 minutes to 1 hour, depending on the temperature of the room.

If you're cooking on a barbecue, make sure the grill is good and hot. Oil the tops of the dough balls and press down to make a disc shape. Place the oiled surface face down on the grill (make sure there is a bit of space between each disc). Cook for 3–4 minutes, or until the grill marks are nice and coloured. Flip and repeat on the other side.

If cooking on a stovetop, add oil to a frying pan over medium heat (a cast iron pan works a treat), then follow the same process as the barbecue method.

FRESH PASTA

Gee, I enjoy eating fresh pasta. It has a lovely, wholesome texture you just don't get with the dried stuff. Making your own might take a few tries until you nail it, but I urge you not to give up. For this recipe, you'll need to get the dough started the day before you want to eat it.

Italians will tell you to use strong 00 flour for pasta making. While there's nothing wrong with it, I prefer a more rustic wholegrain version. You'll need a pasta machine and a fair bit of bench space.

If you've taken the time to make fresh pasta, what's the point of drowning it in a thick, rich sauce? You want the flavour of the flour to shine through so keep things simple. The following is just a guide — sometimes cheese, cracked pepper and olive oil can be just as satisfying.

SERVES 4

2 tablespoons olive oil
1 small–medium-sized onion,
   coarsely chopped
1 long red chilli,
   coarsely chopped
2–3 garlic cloves, crushed
best quality olive oil,
   for dressing
3 handfuls flat-leaf (Italian)
   parsley, coarsely chopped
3 handfuls basil,
   coarsely chopped
freshly grated
   parmesan cheese

PASTA
600 g (1 lb 5 oz/4 cups)
   freshly milled flour, plus
   extra for dusting
2 teaspoons salt
8 egg yolks

To make the pasta, place the flour, salt and egg yolks in a mixing bowl with 200 ml (7 fl oz) of water and mix to form a dough. Knead the dough until smooth and elastic, then place in an oiled bowl, cover and refrigerate overnight.

Use a pasta machine to roll the dough into long thin sheets. Flour the sheets well and cut into 2 cm (¾ inch) thick strips (a small, sharp knife is good for this). You can hang the pasta in the kitchen somewhere to dry for a few hours, but I like to roll and cook straight away as it makes less mess and takes up less space. The fresh pasta will take about 2 minutes to cook in boiling salted water.

To make the topping, add the oil to a large frying pan over medium heat and fry the onion, chilli and garlic for 3–4 minutes until lovely and fragrant, watching closely so the garlic doesn't burn (if you burn the garlic, start again!). Meanwhile, cook the pasta in boiling water, drain and dress with the best quality olive oil you have in the house. Throw the pasta into the frying pan and turn off the heat.

Finish with the chopped herbs, mix through some parmesan cheese and serve.

AUNTIE SUSAN'S LEMON MYRTLE CAKE

For as long as I can remember, my Auntie Susan has baked the most amazing cakes. For years I tried to get her to give me a book with all her recipes. Though I'm still waiting for that book, she shares my passion for native foods and has developed this recipe for me. It's a super simple cake packed with flavour.

SERVES 8

155 g (5½ oz/1 cup)
    macadamia nuts
180 g (6½ oz) butter
150 g (5½ oz) sugar
2 eggs, at room temperature
2 teaspoons baking powder
1 teaspoon bicarbonate of
    soda (baking soda)
300 g (10½ oz/2 cups)
    freshly milled flour
185 ml (6 fl oz/¾ cup)
    buttermilk
2 teaspoons dried
    lemon myrtle
edible flowers,
    to decorate (optional)

ICING
3 egg whites
210 g (7½ oz) caster
    (superfine) sugar
210 g (7½ oz) butter
2 teaspoons dried
    lemon myrtle

NOTE: *Most supermarkets stock lemon myrtle, and it's a cinch to order online. You can also use lemon myrtle teabags – just remove the leaves from the bag and grind them to a fine consistency. This icing can be used for any cake or muffin. Substitute lemon myrtle with any flavour you like.*

Preheat the oven to 160°C (320°F). Grease a 20 cm (8 in) round cake tin and line the base and side with baking paper.

Spread the macadamia nuts evenly on a baking tray and roast for 12 minutes, or until golden brown, then set aside to cool. Turn the oven up to 170°C (340°F).

Using an electric mixer fitted with the paddle attachment, beat the butter until smooth. Add the sugar and cream the two ingredients for 5 minutes, or until light and fluffy. Add 1 egg at a time, making sure the previous one is incorporated before adding the next. Beat for a further 5 minutes.

In a food processor, blitz the macadamia nuts to form a rough breadcrumb consistency. Add the remaining ingredients, except the edible flowers, and the nuts to the butter mixture and beat until smooth. Pour into the cake tin and bake for 40–45 minutes, or until lightly golden. Gently press on the top of the cake – if it bounces back, it's ready. Remove from the oven and let it cool for 10 minutes before turning out onto a wire rack to cool further.

To make the icing, fill a medium saucepan one-third full of water and place over medium heat. Bring to a light simmer. Put the egg whites and sugar into a stainless steel bowl. Using a whisk, briefly mix until the sugar has been incorporated. Place the bowl over the simmering water to create a double boiler and, stirring constantly, heat the mixture until the sugar has dissolved.

Using an electric mixer or hand-held electric beaters, whisk the egg mixture at high speed for 10–12 minutes; it will become white, glossy and thick. Keep whisking until the mixture is cool.

Switch to a paddle attachment if you have one, then mix on medium speed, adding the butter in four batches. Beat until thick and creamy, then add the lemon myrtle and stir until combined. Spatula onto the cake with enthusiasm and decorate with edible flowers, if using.

SHORTCRUST PASTRY

This short, sweet pastry is a great ally to have in the freezer for a variety of tarts, such as the pear and almond number on page 176.

such as the pear and almond number on page 176.

MAKES APPROXIMATELY 1 KG (2 LB 4 OZ)

250 g (9 oz) butter
200 g (7 oz) sugar
500 g (1 lb 2 oz/3⅓ cups)
   freshly milled flour
½ teaspoon salt
2 eggs

Use an electric mixer fitted with the paddle attachment to beat the butter for 3 minutes, or until soft. Add the sugar and beat for a further 5 minutes until the mixture is well combined, pale and fluffy. It's important to mix the sugar and butter well for a good quality pastry.

Add the flour, salt and eggs and mix on medium speed for 4 minutes, or until completely combined into a dough.

Divide the dough into two. Shape each half into a flat square and cover with plastic wrap. Refrigerate overnight before use, or place in the freezer where it will last for up to 1 month.

DOUGHNUTS

I first made these winning doughnuts with David Coomer at the Perth restaurant Star Anise. I like a traditional ring-shaped doughnut, though you can also use this recipe to make balls and fill them with custard, or bake the dough in a tin for a brioche loaf.

MAKES 10–12

185 ml (6 fl oz/¾ cup) milk
1½ tablespoons sugar
5 egg yolks
20 g (¾ oz) fresh yeast
375 g (13 oz/2½ cups) freshly
    milled flour
110 g (3¾ oz) butter, softened
vegetable oil, for deep-frying

CINNAMON SUGAR
110 g (3¾ oz/½ cup) caster
    (superfine) sugar
1¼ teaspoons
    ground cinnamon

In a small saucepan over low heat, gently warm the milk to roughly 30°C (85°F). Mix in the sugar and stir until it has dissolved. Add the egg yolks and yeast and mix through.

Place the flour in the bowl of an electric mixer fitted with the dough hook. Start the mixer on low speed, add the milk mixture and a pinch of salt and mix for 8 minutes. Turn the mixer up to medium speed and add one-third of the butter. Once it's almost all mixed in, add the next third of butter, repeat, then add the final third. When fully combined, the dough should be shiny and smooth.

Place the dough in a lightly oiled bowl and tend the garden or head to the pub for a cheeky beer while it proves and doubles in volume (about 1½ hours).

Knock back the dough and roll it into a rectangle about 2 cm (¾ inch) thick. Use a ring cutter to cut out individual doughnuts – about 8 cm (3¼ inches) is a good diameter. Make the holes by poking your finger in the middle of each doughnut while the cutter is still pressed into the dough, and wriggling it around to make a circle about 2.5 cm (1 inch) in diameter. Leftover dough can be re-rolled for more hot doughnut-making action. Place the doughnuts onto a lightly oiled tray and leave to prove for 1 hour.

Pour vegetable oil into a deep-fryer or large saucepan until about one-third full and heat to 180°C (350°F). If you don't have a cooking thermometer to test the temp, drop a small piece of dough into the oil – when it turns golden after 30 seconds, the oil is the right temperature. Working in batches, carefully place the doughnuts into the oil, being sure not to add too many at once so they're not fighting for real estate. Once the underside of a frying doughnut is golden, flip it and keep frying until both sides are gorgeous and golden. Drain well on paper towel and repeat with the remaining doughnuts.

While the doughnuts are draining and cooling slightly, mix the caster sugar and cinnamon together. Dust the doughnuts until generously coated with cinnamon sugar and serve warm.

DIY dairy means you can easily trace the provenance of the natural raw product; it eliminates all the wasteful packaging that comes with store-bought dairy products; and it gives people a real sense of joy and pride when they serve homemade goodies to friends. Most importantly of all, it's really simple to make.

It's slightly embarrassing to admit but I'd been a chef for about six years before I made fresh butter for the first time. I was at the Greenhouse restaurant in Perth, and owner and mate Joost Bakker had insisted we make our own butter from grass-fed cream. I told him he was dreaming, but he forced me to come round with his constant reminders. And I've never looked back!

Homemade dairy products are now a staple in my kitchen and sourcing the right milk is very important. I want to make sure that my dairy comes from happy cows grazing in open paddocks. Grass-fed dairy is not only delicious, it's also high in nutrients and vitamins. One of these vitamins is K2, which is crucial for distributing calcium evenly around our bones and teeth. It's easy to find information online about grass-fed dairy, its many benefits and the best local products in your area.

FRESH CHEESE

MAKES ABOUT 200 G (7 OZ)

When you have beautiful milk from grass-fed cows it's a real pleasure to make a simple ricotta-style cheese. It's also a great way to use up milk approaching its use-by date that looks like it won't be consumed otherwise. You'll need a cooking thermometer on hand for this recipe.

Be sure to reserve the whey once the cheese is made. This protein-rich product is excellent in breads, desserts and sauces. This recipe can also be made with fresh goat's or sheep's milk.

2.5 litres (87 fl oz/10 cups) full-cream (whole) milk
90 ml (3 fl oz) white vinegar
pinch of sea salt

Heat the milk in a medium saucepan over medium–high heat to 90°C (195°F), stirring with a wooden spoon. While the milk is warming, line a colander with muslin (cheesecloth) or a thin tea towel (dish towel) and place over a bowl. As the milk reaches 90°C (195°F), quickly stir in the vinegar.

The milk will split and coagulate. Turn off the heat. Use a large slotted spoon to take out the curds and gently layer them on the muslin. Leave to drain for about 10 minutes. Put the curds in a bowl and mix through a pinch of sea salt. Store the cheese curds and the whey in separate airtight containers in the fridge. Both will keep for about 1 week.

NOTE: Yields for these recipes will vary from season to season, depending on what the dairy cows have been eating. When lush green grass is plentiful, the fat content in the milk can be up near 60%. Butter made from this milk is high in fat and a bright yellow colour. At other times of the year, when the cows have less green grass to eat and more hay, the fat will be down to 30% or 40%. Yields will be lower and the butter will be paler in hue.

SOUR CREAM, BUTTERMILK & BUTTER

To make butter, you need to make buttermilk. And to make buttermilk, you need to make sour cream. I know this sounds like a huge effort, but it's really not. Once you do it a couple of times you should find the whole thing to be a cathartic, rewarding experience.

SOUR CREAM

MAKES ABOUT 1.4 KG (3 LB 2 OZ)

I like to refrigerate a quarter of the sour cream for jazzing up nachos, roasted vegetables and desserts and use the rest for butter-related activities.

1.25 litres (44 fl oz/5 cups) high-fat cream
150 g (5½ oz) crème fraîche

Mix the cream and crème fraîche together in a bowl and transfer to a large glass jar, making sure none of the mixture is stuck to the sides of the jar (any mixture on the sides will start culturing faster than the rest and we don't want that).

Cover the top with a tea towel (dish towel) and hold it in place with a rubber band. Place the cream in the pantry for 24 hours to kickstart the culturing process, then refrigerate for a further 7 days.

The cream should now be thick, and smell a little like blue cheese. Use a spatula to scrape the cream from the jar and give it a good stir.

Congratulations! You now have homemade sour cream that will keep for up to 1 week in the fridge in an airtight container.

BUTTERMILK

Buttermilk is great to use in cakes, pancakes and salad dressings, and to brine chicken before deep-frying. After you have reserved any sour cream for a future nacho session, the rest can be churned into butter.

Scrape the sour cream into the bowl of an electric mixer fitted with the paddle attachment. Start the mixer on low speed and, as the cream starts to thicken, increase the speed to high. The mix will get very thick.

It will all come together into one piece. When this happens, be very alert that it is about to split into buttermilk and butter and things can get messy. When you see it is about to split, cover the mixer with a towel to stop getting buttermilk everywhere.

Once the cream has split, keep the mixer going until the sound changes from a whipping noise to a splashing noise. As soon as this happens, turn the mixer off. If you keep it mixing, the buttermilk will be incorporated back into the butter.

Pour the mixture into a sieve over a bowl to catch the buttermilk. Because the cream is so sour, the buttermilk will only keep in the fridge for about 2 days. If you want a less sour cream and buttermilk, you can process the cream after 3–4 days of culturing in the fridge (instead of 7). Set the solid butter aside.

BUTTER

Soft butter is one of those must-have staples, next to your salt and olive oil.

Fill a large bowl with iced water. Take small handfuls of the solid butter and squeeze it into balls, trying to squash out all the buttermilk. If you have some old butter paddles lying around the house (because who doesn't?) you can use them instead of your hands.

Place the butter balls into the iced water. Once all the buttermilk has been squeezed out, dry well on a tea towel (dish towel).

The butter is now ready. I usually put half of it straight into a sealed container and into the fridge to use for cooking. The other half I mix in a bowl with flaky sea salt to be slathered on toast.

The butter will keep in the fridge for about 2 weeks.

YOGHURT, LABNE & WHEY

I had played around with making yoghurt a bit earlier on in my cooking life but nowhere near as seriously as I did at Greenhouse. These days I can't get enough of the creamy, delicious homemade stuff, so I always have some on hand. Labne is one of the easiest cheeses you can make at home, and whey is a terrific by-product that has multiple uses in the kitchen.

YOGHURT

MAKES ABOUT 2 KG (4 LB 8 OZ)

Fresh yoghurt is so easy to make and much cheaper than buying it from the shops. I like to make it myself because I can choose where the milk has come from and I end up with plenty of whey left over to use in desserts and sauces. You just need a small amount of yoghurt to start off with to make a much larger batch.

I like to use raw milk for this as it's much higher in nutrients and the flavour is better. The cooking process of the milk will make it completely safe. If you can't get raw milk or if you're not comfortable using it, biodynamic or organic milk is fine. Be sure to save at least 130 g (4½ oz/½ cup) of the yoghurt to start your next batch.

2 litres (70 fl oz/8 cups) best quality
   full-cream (whole) milk
130 g (4½ oz/½ cup) full-fat plain yoghurt

Pour the milk into a heavy-based saucepan and place it over medium heat. Slowly bring the milk to the boil and just before it starts to bubble like crazy, turn it down to a simmer. It's perfect if you get slight bubbles every now and then and a steady stream of steam. Stir often with a wooden spoon, making sure the milk skin doesn't catch on the side of the pan. If it's starting to catch, place a metal tray on the burner and put the pan on it to soften the heat. Leave to reduce slightly for about 30 minutes. Turn off and leave to cool to about 35–40°C (95–105°F).

Add the yoghurt. Mix well. Pass through a fine sieve into a container or jar. Leave on the kitchen bench for 24 hours for the yoghurt to set. If it's the middle of winter and freezing cold, place it in one of the warmer spots around the house.

Line a large sieve with muslin (cheesecloth), or a thin tea towel (dish towel) if you don't have muslin, and place the sieve over a bowl. Steadily pour in the yoghurt. Cover and put in the fridge.

As soon as the yoghurt has dropped in temperature it's ready to eat, although at this early stage it will be a bit runny. I like to leave it to drain for another 24 hours, at which point the yoghurt will have thickened nicely and there'll be lots of whey.

LABNE & WHEY

Labne is a simple, fresh, wholesome cheese and I always have some in the fridge and on my menus. It can be mixed with wattleseed or vanilla and served with fresh fruit; it can be served plain on the side with roasted vegetables; or in salads as you would use feta. Whey has a lovely acidic flavour, is full of protein and is good in breads, desserts and sauces.

Place a sieve over a large bowl and place a piece of muslin (cheesecloth), or a thin tea towel (dish towel) if you don't have muslin, in the sieve, leaving no gaps. Spoon your fresh yoghurt onto the cloth. Place in the fridge and leave for 48 hours. The whey will drain into the bowl and the yoghurt will thicken to labne.

The labne will keep for up to 1 week in the fridge in an airtight container, or you could marinate it in a sterilised jar filled with good quality olive oil and 1 tablespoon of peppercorns.

Be sure to keep all of the whey that drains from the labne. It will keep in the fridge for up to 1 week but can be frozen and stored for a few months.

2.
FERMENTING, BRINING & PICKLING

GREEN
CORIANDER
SEED.

Fermenting, brining and pickling are great ways to preserve produce, make the most of abundance and turn day-to-day cooking into an exciting activity. You can never have a boring meal if you've got a pantry full of pickles at your disposal. Leftover rice? Add a handful of pickled vegetables to it and dinner's ready. Is that chicken from last night looking a bit lonely? Add some fermented chilli paste for some extra heat.

Glass jars are terrific for storing, preserving and fermenting food, and through re-use they help to minimise waste in a big way. My kitchen is full of them. I use 1 litre (35 fl oz/4 cup) jars for most fermented foods, even though some of the recipes only half-fill the jars. Some of the foods (particularly the chilli paste) need room to breathe. Also, using the same-sized jars keeps things streamlined in the kitchen.

It's really important the jars are washed and sterilised thoroughly to kill any nasty bacteria lurking in them that will give you a dodgy stomach or worse. It also stops flavour crossovers. For example, if you have used a jar for chutney and don't sterilise it before using it to store jam, you might end up with a breakfast spread that tastes like turmeric and onion.

To sterilise your jars, preheat your oven to 180°C (350°F). Fill your sink with hot water and wash your jars and lids well. Leave the jars to drain on the bench before placing them on a rack in the oven for 15 minutes. Dry the lids with a clean tea towel (dish towel) while the jars are heating up (it's important that the tea towel is clean – you don't want bacteria to find its way onto the lids). Carefully remove the jars from the oven and leave to cool. They are now ready to use any way you see fit.

When filling your jars, be sure to leave at least 1 cm (½ inch) of space at the top to make room for the gases as your fermented foods come to life. Otherwise, you'll have a sticky, smelly mess (which I've cleaned up many times). Not fun.

FERMENTED CABBAGE

Who doesn't love a crusty roll filled with a sausage or crunchy vegetables and a healthy helping of sauerkraut? As cabbage has such a high water content, there's often some brining liquid left over. You can use this for the Fermented Cauliflower (see page 48), so it's not a bad idea to make both recipes at the same time.

USE A 1 LITRE (35 FL OZ/4 CUP) JAR

1 kg (2 lb 4 oz) white cabbage
3 teaspoons salt
1 teaspoon raw
   (demerara) sugar

Peel back the outer leaves of the cabbage and set these aside for later use. Cut the cabbage into quarters, remove the core and finely shred everything else.

Place the shredded cabbage in a bowl with the salt and sugar. Using your hands, really get in there and bruise up the cabbage. This helps the salt and sugar draw out all the cabbage liquid and start the brine. Leave it to sit for about 1 hour, giving it the occasional stir and prod.

Firmly press the cabbage into a sterilised jar, leaving no air pockets. Pour over the brine, let things settle down and top up the jar with more brine, leaving at least 1 cm (½ inch) of space. Cut the reserved outer cabbage leaves into rounds slightly larger than the top of the jar. Press these into the top of the jar and cover with more liquid. Cover the jar with muslin (cheesecloth) or a clean kitchen cloth, using a rubber band or string to hold it in place. The cloth will let air in but keep dust and curious insects out.

Leave the jar on the shelf out of direct sunlight for 4–8 days, depending on how funky you like your ferment. The season will affect the fermentation time as well: you'll need a longer ferment in cold weather and a shorter one in the warmer months. It's important to release the fermentation gas that builds up, so the jar doesn't explode. You'll need to do this on a daily basis. No-one wants an exploding jar in the house.

Once the cabbage is at a stage that suits your taste, screw on the lid and store it in the fridge, where it will last for months.

FERMENTED CHILLI PASTE

A handy staple to keep in the fridge, this delicious chilli paste is great
with stir-fries or noodles or served on the side with barbecued chicken.

USE A 1 LITRE (35 FL OZ/4 CUP) JAR

500 g (1 lb 2 oz) large
  red chillies
1½ tablespoons salt
½ teaspoon raw
  (demerara) sugar

Wash the chillies and slice the stems off. Give them a rough chop
and mix with the salt and sugar in a bowl. Leave them to cure for
about 1 hour and then blend into a fine purée.

Transfer the mix to a sterilised jar. It will only fill the jar a third of
the way, but it needs plenty of room to breathe. Cover with muslin
(cheesecloth) or a clean kitchen cloth held in place by a rubber
band or string, and leave on a shelf out of direct sunlight for 4 days.
The juice will separate from the purée, so give it a mix each day.

Once ready, transfer to a smaller airtight jar and refrigerate. It will
keep for at least a month.

FERMENTED CAULIFLOWER

Fantastic as both a finger food and a side dish to cut through rich meats,
this fermented cauli is also delicious mixed with fresh herbs and quinoa.

USE A 1 LITRE (35 FL OZ/4 CUP) JAR

600 g (1 lb 5 oz)
  cauliflower, stalk and
  florets roughly diced
2 teaspoons salt
1 large pinch of raw
  (demerara) sugar

Put the cauliflower in a container with the salt and sugar. Place
the lid on and shake it really hard. Like, REALLY hard. This will
bruise the cauliflower and start the fermenting process. Put the
mixture into a sterilised jar and press down firmly. Pour over enough
water to cover the cauliflower (or you can use leftover cabbage
brine from page 46 if you have some).

Cover the jar with muslin (cheesecloth) or a clean kitchen cloth,
held in place by a rubber band or string. Store out of direct sunlight.
Cauliflower has the same 4–8 day ferment time as the cabbage.
Remember to release the fermentation gases daily. After the
ferment, cover with an airtight lid and store the jar in the fridge,
where it will last for months.

FERMENTED BEANS

As well as making a crunchy side for braised meats and Asian rice dishes, these beans are a nutritious snack for any time of the day. Perfect for a school lunchbox.

USE A 1 LITRE (35 FL OZ/4 CUP) JAR

500 g (1 lb 2 oz/6 cups)
   green beans, halved
   and stem-end removed
1½ teaspoons salt
1 pinch of raw
   (demerara) sugar

Put the beans in a container with the salt and sugar. Place the lid on and shake it hard. This will bruise the beans and start the fermenting process. Put the mixture into a sterilised jar, press down firmly and pour over enough water to cover the beans.

Cover the jar with muslin (cheesecloth) or a clean kitchen cloth held in place by a rubber band or string. Store out of direct sunlight for 4–8 days, releasing the gases daily. After the ferment, cover with an airtight lid and refrigerate; it will last for months.

APPLE & POMEGRANATE VINEGAR

It takes a bloody long time to ferment vinegar but gee, it's worth it. Luckily, it only takes a few minutes to mix, and then you can almost forget about it. I like to use fruit juice, as it makes a floral, mellow-tasting vinegar that's terrific drizzled over salads and added to braises and soups.

USE A 2 LITRE (70 FL OZ/8 CUP) JAR

1 litre (35 fl oz/4 cups) fresh
   apple juice
300 ml (10½ fl oz)
   pomegranate juice
100 ml (3½ fl oz) apple cider
   vinegar with live 'mother'

NOTE: *The 'mother' of the vinegar is a mix of proteins, enzymes and friendly bacteria. These vinegars can be found at all good health food stores.*

Fresh juice is needed to make this vinegar – make sure any fleshy bits are removed by passing it through a sieve first. Mix the juice with the vinegar and pour into a large sterilised jar – a 2 litre (70 fl oz/8 cup) capacity jar is perfect. Be sure to leave a gap at the top so it can breathe.

Screw on a lid and store in the back of the pantry, opening to release the pressure once a week for the first 4 weeks. From then on, once a month is fine. The vinegar will take from 3 to 6 months to develop, depending on the ambient temperature. The longer you leave it, the more tart it will become.

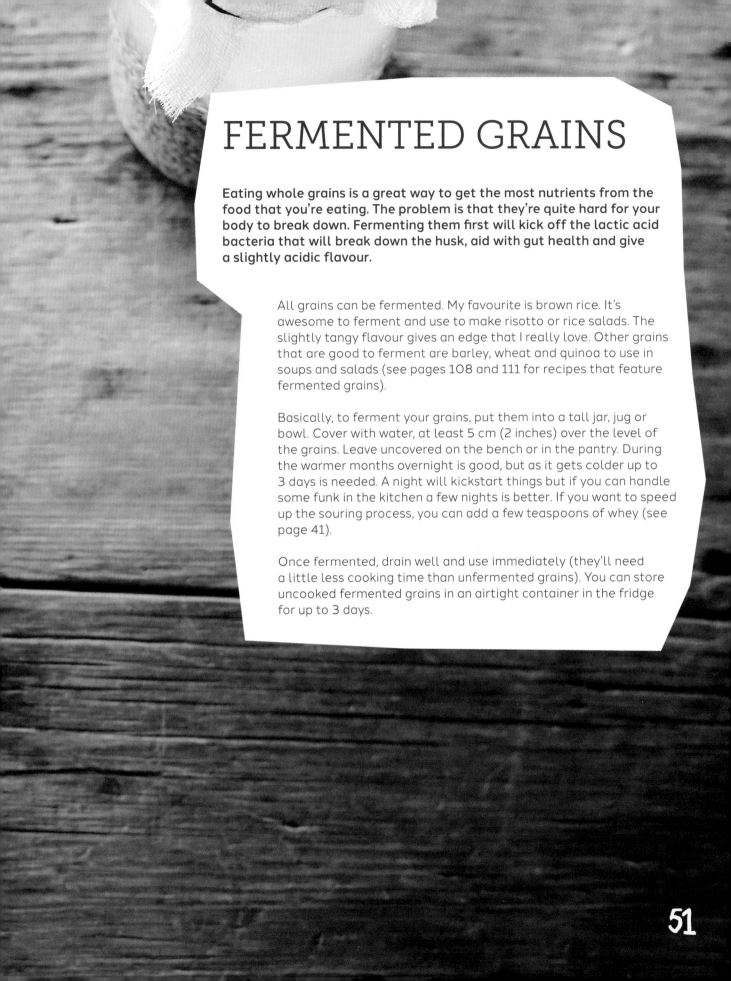

FERMENTED GRAINS

Eating whole grains is a great way to get the most nutrients from the food that you're eating. The problem is that they're quite hard for your body to break down. Fermenting them first will kick off the lactic acid bacteria that will break down the husk, aid with gut health and give a slightly acidic flavour.

All grains can be fermented. My favourite is brown rice. It's awesome to ferment and use to make risotto or rice salads. The slightly tangy flavour gives an edge that I really love. Other grains that are good to ferment are barley, wheat and quinoa to use in soups and salads (see pages 108 and 111 for recipes that feature fermented grains).

Basically, to ferment your grains, put them into a tall jar, jug or bowl. Cover with water, at least 5 cm (2 inches) over the level of the grains. Leave uncovered on the bench or in the pantry. During the warmer months overnight is good, but as it gets colder up to 3 days is needed. A night will kickstart things but if you can handle some funk in the kitchen a few nights is better. If you want to speed up the souring process, you can add a few teaspoons of whey (see page 41).

Once fermented, drain well and use immediately (they'll need a little less cooking time than unfermented grains). You can store uncooked fermented grains in an airtight container in the fridge for up to 3 days.

CHARRED & PICKLED ONIONS

It's pretty common to see 'burnt onions' on menus these days. This is my version: after the onions are charred, a light pickling rounds off proceedings and adds depth of flavour. The pickling mixture cures the onion, diminishing its strong oniony taste.

These are great on a plate of cured meats, in a toasted sandwich or in a grain salad. The vinegar-oil mix can be used a few times and makes a good dressing for roasted vegetables and salads.

USE A 1 LITRE (35 FL OZ/4 CUP) JAR

2 brown onions
100 ml (3½ fl oz) olive oil,
  plus extra for frying
150 ml (5 fl oz) apple cider
  vinegar, ideally with live
  'mother' (see page 49)
1 teaspoon salt
1 teaspoon honey

Cut the onions in half, root to shoot, leaving the skin on. Place a large heavy-based frying pan over medium–high heat and add a generous splash of oil. Fry the onions on their cut side, pressing down with another pan or pot to make sure all the flesh is coming into contact with the hot surface. You pretty much want to burn the onions so cook them for about 8 minutes until they're black, but still firm and holding their shape.

Turn off the heat and, when cool enough to handle, peel away the onion skins and discard. The layers of the onions will come apart easily into small cups. Place them into a mixing bowl while still warm and add the 100 ml (3½ fl oz) olive oil, vinegar, salt and honey. Stir well.

Leave the mixture out on the bench for at least 1 hour, stirring often. Transfer to a sterilised jar and refrigerate; they'll keep in the fridge for 2–3 weeks.

BRINED CHICKEN & FISH

There are many benefits to brining chicken and fish fillets. It helps the salt permeate the flesh so it's seasoned beautifully the whole way through, not just on the surface – and it keeps fish and chicken fresh for a few more days. So if you go fishing and catch more than you need that night, brining is the perfect solution. I use a 5% salt ratio for my brine. All you have to do is dissolve the salt in the water and it's ready to go.

SERVES 4

BRINED CHICKEN
1 whole chicken, about 1.2 kg
   (2 lb 10 oz)
250 g (9 oz) salt

BRINED FISH
100 g (3½ oz) salt
600–700 g (1 lb 5 oz–
   1 lb 9 oz) firm white
   fish fillets

Clear a big space in the fridge. Place the chicken in a large stockpot, cover with 5 litres (175 fl oz/20 cups) of water and add the salt. Cover with a lid and refrigerate for at least 6 hours or overnight (chicken is firmer than fish and can be left to brine overnight). Once brined, drain well on paper towel, discarding the brine, then cook the chicken as per normal. Brined chicken will keep in an airtight container in the fridge for up to 1 week.

If you're brining fish, place 2 litres (70 fl oz/8 cups) of water in a large saucepan or stockpot, add the salt and submerge the fillets in the brine. Leave the fish in the fridge for 2–4 hours (if you leave it too long, it will become mushy). Once brined, drain well on paper towel, discarding the brine, then cook the fish as per normal. Brined fish will keep in an airtight container in the fridge for up to 5 days.

BRINED SHAVED VEGETABLES

This is a no-nonsense way to brine vegetables for crunchy, fresh salads. Simply dress with good olive oil and mix with herbs and salad leaves.

MAKES 1 KG (2 LB 4 OZ)

1 lemon
100 g (3½ oz) salt
1 kg (2 lb 4 oz) mixed
   vegetables (I like to use
   carrots, beetroot (beets),
   radish and celery), finely
   shaved on a mandolin

Peel the lemon and cut the peel into long thin strips. In a large saucepan, dissolve the salt in 1.5 litres (52 fl oz/6 cups) of water. Juice the lemon and add the juice to the brine. Place the shaved vegetables in the brine, along with the strips of lemon peel. Mix through and press down on the vegetables until submerged. Refrigerate for 2–4 hours; they will crisp up and become well seasoned. Strain the veg, discarding the liquid. They will keep for 4–5 days in an airtight container in the fridge.

PRESERVED LEMONS

One of the best things about the Aussie backyard is the good old lemon tree; I don't think there's a neighbourhood that doesn't have one. You can rarely get through every lemon on a tree when they're in season, so preserving is a great way to use them up before they start dropping off and rotting on the ground.

The flavour of a preserved lemon is very different from a fresh one and they make a top addition to salads, dressings and tagines.

USE A 2 LITRE (70 FL OZ/8 CUP) JAR

20 lemons
400 g (14 oz) salt
3 cinnamon sticks
1 tablespoon coriander seeds
1 tablespoon ground cumin
1 teaspoon black peppercorns
1 teaspoon whole cloves
10 cardamom pods
5 dried chillies
pinch of saffron

Flex your squeezing arm and juice half of the lemons. Cut the rest into quarters, ALMOST all the way through, starting at the top and leaving 2 cm (¾ inch) of each lemon intact at the bottom to hold it together. Place the almost-quartered lemons into a large mixing bowl with the salt and spices. Mix really well, pressing and studding the salt and spice into the lemons.

Squash the lemons into a sterilised jar. Pour in the juice and squash the lemons down even more. You might want to press a small piece of baking paper on top of the lemons to make sure none bob above the liquid. If the lemons weren't the juiciest fruit and there's not enough liquid, you can top it up with some water. Seal the jar with a lid and leave the lemons in a cool, dark place for 3 months.

These preserved beauties should last you at least until the next lemon season rolls around.

PICKLED VEGETABLES

This is a basic pickle recipe that can be used for all sorts of vegetables. Carrots, turnips, beetroot (beets), radishes and cucumbers are some of my favourites. Any type of vinegar can be used, although this recipe is based on a good quality white vinegar. If you're using something different, taste it when the pickling liquid is just made – add more sugar if it's too sharp or more vinegar if it's too sweet. Easy. Make the pickle to your taste – there are no rules.

USE A 1 LITRE (35 FL OZ/4 CUP) JAR

500 ml (17 fl oz/2 cups) white vinegar
100 g (3½ oz) raw (demerara) sugar
1½ tablespoons salt
20 baby carrots
20 baby turnips

Combine the vinegar, sugar and salt with 250 ml (9 fl oz/1 cup) of water in a medium saucepan and place over medium heat. Bring to the boil and start stirring. Once the sugar and salt have dissolved, turn off the heat.

You now have a pickling liquid you can pour over vegetables. If you're pickling hard vegetables, such as the carrots and turnips here, you can pour the liquid over while it's still hot. However, for softer vegetables, such as cucumber and radish, cool the pickling liquid down first.

Pickle your vegetables in sterilised jars or airtight containers, making sure that the vegetables are completely submerged in the liquid. These whole baby carrots and turnips will need 2–3 weeks' pickling time. The smaller the cut, the quicker the pickle. For example, if you shave the carrots and turnips into strips with a vegetable peeler, these will only take 1 week to pickle. Whole chillies will take 4 weeks, but if you cut them diagonally into strips, they will take only 2 weeks.

You can add other flavours to the basic pickle, too. For instance, I like to add sliced ginger when pickling cucumbers, mustard seeds with carrots, and thyme and bay leaves with beetroot. It's all up to you, so play around with different flavours.

Leftover pickling liquid can be stored in the fridge and will last for months. Pickled vegetables can be left in the pantry out of direct sunlight or stored in the fridge. In the fridge there's little chance of spoiling but if everything's sterilised and covered with liquid, you shouldn't have problems anyway. Pickled vegetables will last at least 2 months on the shelf unopened, and about the same amount of time in the fridge once opened.

PICKLED FENNEL FLOWERS

Fennel grows wild all over the place, in many parts of the world, its flowers fragrant and full of flavour. The only problem is that they're also quite fibrous and not overly pleasant to eat raw.

I got the idea to pickle fennel flowers and green coriander seeds after spending a day in the kitchen at Noma in Copenhagen. These flowers are great with pork, chicken or fish, and can be added to desserts with tropical fruits such as pineapple, mango or papaya – the floral acidic flavour helps to cut through the sweetness.

You can also extract pollen from the flowers by placing them in a paper bag and giving it a shake. The pollen that collects in the bottom of the bag can be sprinkled over both sweet and savoury dishes for a bit of delicious fun.

USE A 500 ML (17 FL OZ/2 CUP) JAR

250 ml (9 fl oz/1 cup) apple cider vinegar with a live 'mother' (see page 49)
125 ml (4 fl oz/½ cup) water
110 g (3¾ oz/½ cup) raw (demerara) sugar
6 pepperberries
2 cups wild fennel flowers, trimmed

NOTE: *Pepperberries can be purchased online from bush food and herb and spice specialists. See page 126 for more information on foraging for ingredients such as wild fennel.*

Pour the vinegar and water into a small saucepan. Add the sugar and pepperberries and place over medium heat. Bring to the boil and stir until the sugar has dissolved. Leave the mix to cool.

Place the fennel flowers in a sterilised jar and gently press them down. Pour over the cooled pickling liquid and press down the flowers again so they're completely submerged. Screw a lid on top and leave to pickle in a cool, dark place for at least 1 week.

These last at least 3 months.

PICKLED GREEN CORIANDER SEEDS

As spring hits and it starts to warm up, the coriander will generally go to seed. I like to pickle the seeds and use them in both sweet and savoury dishes to add a fresh zingy hit. I use them on salads, in pork dishes and even lemony desserts.

One of the benefits of growing your own herbs and vegetables is being able to use all of the plant all of the year. When your coriander goes to seed, harvest them and pickle them.

USE A 500 ML (17 FL OZ/2 CUP) JAR

250 ml (9 fl oz/1 cup) apple cider vinegar, ideally with a live 'mother' (see page 49)
110 g (3¾ oz/½ cup) raw (demerara) sugar
60 g (2 oz/1 cup) green coriander seeds
coriander flowers

NOTE: *To source coriander seeds, you'll need to grow your own flowers or find a friend who does. The seeds are pickled in bunches on the stem.*

Pour the vinegar and 125 ml (4 fl oz/½ cup) of water into a small saucepan and place over medium heat. Add the sugar and bring to the boil. Stir until the sugar has dissolved, then remove from the heat and leave to cool.

Place the coriander seeds and flowers into a sterilised preserving jar. Pour the cool liquid into the jar and press the seeds and flowers down so there are none sticking their heads above the liquid. Seal the jar with a lid and leave in a cool, dark place for 2 weeks.

These pickled seeds will last for at least 6 months.

PICKLED HERRING

Herring is one of my favourite fish – they're really fun to catch and they taste sensational. I like to serve pickled herring with toast and aioli for a great starter or snack. This recipe works well with sardines, octopus and mussels, too.

SERVES 4–6 AS A SNACK

2 teaspoons coriander seeds
2 teaspoons fennel seeds
2 teaspoons black
  peppercorns
olive oil
1 red onion, sliced into 5 mm
  (¼ inch) thick pieces
1 carrot, sliced as thinly as
  possible into rounds
½ fennel bulb, sliced into
  5 mm (¼ inch) thick pieces
400 ml (14 fl oz)
  red wine vinegar
75 g (2¾ oz/⅓ cup) raw
  (demerara) sugar
1 tablespoon salt
4 thyme sprigs
4 flat-leaf (Italian)
  parsley sprigs
2 bay leaves
2 tablespoons vegetable oil
6 herring, gutted, scaled
  and filleted

Place a medium frying pan over medium heat and lightly toast the coriander seeds, fennel seeds and peppercorns until fragrant. Add a splash of olive oil to the pan and when it heats up a bit, add the onion, carrot and fennel. Cook for 1 minute, stirring constantly. Add the vinegar and 100 ml (3½ fl oz) of water. Bring to the boil, then add the sugar, salt and herbs. Simmer for 5 minutes, then turn off the heat.

Place a large frying pan over high heat. Once the pan is hot, add the vegetable oil and place the fish skin side down. Cook for 2 minutes and turn off the heat. Place the fish into a snug dish, trying not to overlap them. Pour over the hot pickling liquid.

Leave to cool on the bench, then cover and put in the fridge. The fish needs at least 4 hours to pickle, but overnight is best. It will keep for about 1 week.

KIMCHI

Kimchi is one of my favourite things to have on the side of a meal (I also love it on grilled cheese toasties). This recipe makes a much larger batch than the other fermented recipes because once you try it, you won't be able to stop eating it.

USE A 2 LITRE (70 FL OZ/8 CUP) JAR

1 large Chinese cabbage
   (wong bok)
2 tablespoons salt
1 teaspoon raw
   (demerara) sugar
10 spring onions (scallions)
2 carrots, thinly shredded
   or coarsely grated
2 apples, grated
4 garlic cloves, finely chopped
5 cm (2 inch) piece ginger,
   peeled and finely chopped
3 teaspoons Fermented Chilli
   Paste (see page 48)

NOTE: *I use my own fermented chilli paste in this kimchi, but you can use a store-bought version if you like.*

Peel back the outer leaves of the cabbage and set these aside for later use. Split the cabbage lengthways, remove the base and cut crossways into slices about 1 cm (½ inch) thick. Put the cabbage into a mixing bowl and add the salt and sugar. Roughly bruise the cabbage by mixing and squeezing with your hands, then leave it to sit. Cut the spring onions in half, save the top halves for drying and thinly slice the rest. Mix the sliced spring onion, carrot, apple, garlic and ginger with the cabbage.

Strain off all the excess liquid from the cabbage mixture and reserve for later. Add the chilli paste and mix through thoroughly. Firmly push the mixture into a sterilised jar. It should just fit into a 2 litre (70 fl oz/8 cup) jar but if it doesn't, add any extra to a small jar. There should be no pockets of air in the jar (or jars). Add the reserved liquid to cover. Cut the reserved outer cabbage leaves into rounds slightly larger than the top of the jar. Press these into the top of the jar and cover with more liquid. Cover with muslin (cheesecloth) or a clean kitchen cloth held in place with a rubber band or string. Store out of direct sunlight for 6–10 days until nicely fermented to your liking.

Seal the jar with a lid and store in the fridge. It will keep for a couple of months, but there's a very good chance you will have used it all by that point anyway.

FERMENTED PEARS

These pears are excellent with cured meats, cheese or roast pork.
You'll need a juicer for this recipe.

USE A 1 LITRE (35 FL OZ/4 CUP) JAR

6 pears (any variety)
2 large pinches of raw
(demerara) sugar

Wash and core the fruit and set 3 pears aside for juicing. Remove the edges of the remaining pears to square them up and cut into nice 5 mm (¼ inch) dice, leaving bits of skin on here and there.

In a mixing bowl, combine the diced pear with the sugar and a pinch of salt. Juice the remaining pears. Place the diced pear into a sterilised jar and pour over the juice. Seal the jar with a lid and leave for 3–4 days out of direct sunlight, stirring each day. When ready, store the pears in the fridge, where they'll keep for 2 weeks. The leftover fermented juice can be added to the Apple and Pomegranate Vinegar (see page 49).

FERMENTED RASPBERRIES

Too often berries go off in the fridge before we get round to eating them. They cost far too much to waste or compost, so I made this recipe to avoid that situation.

This fermented purée makes a great summer drink with a big splash of sparkling wine or soda water or both. It's also great to dress up a fruit salad or to finish a sauce for game meats.

USE AN OLD 300 ML (10½ FL OZ) JAM JAR

250 g (9 oz/2 cups)
raspberries
1 tablespoon raw
(demerara) sugar
1 tablespoon water

NOTE: *You can use any type of berry here, not just raspberries.*

Put all the ingredients into a bowl and smash together into a big, bright mess. Pour into a sterilised jam jar, cover with muslin (cheesecloth) or a clean kitchen cloth held in place with a rubber band or string, and leave for 2–3 days out of direct sunlight until bubbly and fermented, giving it a mix each day.

Store the purée in the fridge in an airtight container where it will keep for 2 weeks.

I've known Joost Bakker since 2009, and was proud to be part of his zero-waste restaurant venture in Melbourne, Brothl. Joost is constantly pushing the boundaries of how we think about food, design and farming and is responsible for leading me towards healthy, sustainable, ethical food that has a minimal impact on the environment.

All kinds of out-there ideas of his – like milling fresh grain, composting, making bone broth, fermentation and foraging – are staple practices for me now. We've worked on many projects together, from pop-up restaurants and small private dinners to talks at schools, television interviews, growing food, and travelling overseas to meet people making cutting-edge equipment. Joost's influence will continue to change the hospitality industry in Australia and around the world.

> 'Worldwide, nutrients are being dumped into landfill. At the same time, food is becoming less nutrient-dense. Limiting organic waste by upcycling these nutrients back into the food system is what Brothl was all about – with core beliefs centring around the promotion of healthy nutrient-rich soils, producing nutrient-rich food.'
> JOOST BAKKER

Many people love the idea of sustainability but put waste reduction in the too-hard basket. Despite lots of goodwill and good intentions, they presume they can't find space in their hectic schedules to live more sustainably. But it's not as difficult and time-consuming as you might think. Every little step, no matter how small, makes a difference. Here are a few easy ways to reduce your food waste and live a healthier, more sustainable lifestyle.

GROWING YOUR OWN

Even though I live in the inner city, with limited backyard space (about 4 square metres of garden bed), I manage to grow plenty of herbs and veggies, which saves me a lot of money and reduces waste. Growing herbs that you use all the time means there are no half-used bunches of herbs going soft and saggy in the fridge. Rather than having to buy a large bunch that you don't need, you can simply harvest the leaves you require for a specific dish from your own garden – no more, no less.

We always have herbs like parsley, sage, rosemary, mint and thyme on the go. Basic things that are easy to grow. We also plant a small seasonal crop of a few veggies and have successfully grown good amounts of tomato, cucumber, celery, radish, zucchini (courgette), broad (fava) beans, peas, pumpkin (winter squash), eggplant (aubergine) and chilli. (We've struggled with leafy greens thanks to some enthusiastic possums next door.) We also have seven old wine kegs that we grow plants like lemon myrtle, curry leaf, chilli, lemon tree, passionfruit vine and capers in. Re-using the kegs looks great and means we can move these plants around when we need to.

Then there's the aquaponics. One night we were up late drinking beers and watching online videos about food, farming and cooking. There was a cool video about using aquaponics to grow food where there were poor growing conditions and pretty ordinary soil. We thought it was great and decided with conviction we would start doing the same thing in Melbourne. And, like most brilliant ideas that spring up after a six-pack, nothing happened. Then I went away on a work trip and came home to find that my housemates had turned a 1000-litre water container into a fish farm and grow bed.

Essentially it pumps water from the tank below up through the stones in the grow bed. We planted it with mint, basil, snow peas (mangetout) and watercress and I got some trout. We had mixed success initially but are now at a good balance and have created a healthy system with plenty of algae for the fish to feed on and loads of nutrients for the plants. We have been eating lots of watercress and mint and are looking forward to the day we can have our first meal of trout from our backyard. The best thing about this system is that it only takes up a small corner of our yard that once did nothing.

We also have a tumble composter, three worm farms, a wood barbecue, and table and chairs to have guests over. This is all in a backyard of about 25 square metres down the side of the house in a heavily populated inner-city suburb. It's amazing how well you can utilise the space you have with a bit of planning.

FERMENTING, BRINING & PICKLING

Of course, when you have an abundance of produce from the backyard veggie patch, nothing need go to waste. There are plenty of ways to preserve your excess herbs and veggies, including fermenting, brining and pickling. For more on these easy techniques as well as some of my favourite recipes, see pages 42–64.

COMPOSTING AT HOME

Inevitably, you won't be able to eat or preserve everything. That's what the compost bin is for. It's a great way to avoid waste and to return nutrients to the soil. Every household should be composting its organic waste so it can be returned to the soil for future crops. Instead, we're using natural gas to manufacture synthetic fertilisers, which makes absolutely no sense – especially when it has been estimated that nearly one-third of landfill is compostable waste.

Even if you're renting, or only have a tiny balcony or courtyard, you can still get composting. A small worm farm is a great way to compost at least some of your waste and they don't smell too bad (you also get amazing 'worm juice' that your garden will go nuts for). Tumble composters are good if you have a little more room and at the other end of the scale there are small machines that can be kept indoors, have zero stink and turn your waste into compost overnight.

DON'T PEEL YOUR VEG

I rarely peel vegetables. Vegetables that are raw and unpeeled or cooked in the skin will always taste better and be higher in vitamins and nutrients. Just give any raw vegetables a quick brush under cold water first to remove any dirt and you'll be sweet. Onions are one of the exceptions but they're still beautiful with their skin on when roasted on coals or in an oven until soft and sweet. Squeeze out the soft centres – they're delicious with meat and in salads.

MAKING STOCK & BROTH

When you've removed the flesh from your fish, chicken or beef, and turned it into a delicious meal, don't bin the bones immediately. Instead, make the most of their health-giving qualities by using them for stocks and broths. For more on broth, including some great waste-saving recipes, see pages 70–89.

USING FRUIT PEELS

Rather than throw your flavoursome fruit peel into the compost, you can use it to add something a little bit different (and delicious) to your meals.

Citrus peels can be dried and powdered and stored in a jar to sprinkle on ice cream or other desserts, or even used in seafood or poultry dishes (see Dried & Powdered, page 93). Dried peach skins can make a beautiful tea, while orange peel left over from juicing is excellent used to flavour a stock for poaching fruits such as rhubarb or apples. Dried apple skins, cut thinly, make a great garnish for an apple crumble or apple pie. Nothing need go to waste.

3.
BROTH

A cure-all in traditional households and the magic ingredient in classic gourmet cuisine, stock or broth made from bones of chicken, beef or fish builds strong bones, assuages sore throats, nurtures the sick, puts vigour in the step and sparkle in the love life – so say grandmothers, midwives and healers. For chefs, stock is the magic elixir for making soul-warming soups and matchless sauces.

Broth was the backbone of Brothl, the no-waste café that Joost Bakker and I established in Melbourne in 2013, which utilised the waste and scraps from other local restaurants to create healthy broths. It is also the backbone of an infinite number of delicious soups.

In this chapter I've given the basic recipes for the straight broths we served at the café – clean-tasting and light and good to enjoy as is – plus suggestions for turning them into hearty meals. They're only suggestions though. Think of broth as a base to which you can add your favourite vegetables, seafood, meat, herbs and noodles. Or, as always, whatever's crying out for attention at the bottom of the fridge.

It's important to use filtered water for making broths whenever possible as there are so many added nasties and bits and pieces in our tap water. To see what I'm talking about, simply put a clean saucepan of water on the stove and reduce it until it's almost all gone. Once it's cool, run a clean towel around the inside of the pan and you'll notice some brownish residue left from the water. It has a weird taste and it can't be good.

CHICKEN BROTH

An excellent source of vitamins, this broth will help you stay fit and healthy and more resistant to viral nasties. It also smells and tastes amazing.

MAKES ABOUT 4 LITRES (140 FL OZ/16 CUPS)

6 garlic cloves, peeled
  and smashed
6 spring onions (scallions),
  top green halves only
5 cm (2 inch) piece ginger,
  scrubbed and chopped
1 teaspoon salt
30 ml (1 fl oz) apple cider
  vinegar, ideally with a live
  'mother' (see page 49)
1 x 1.2 kg (2 lb 10 oz) chicken

Pour 5 litres (175 fl oz/20 cups) of water into a large saucepan or stockpot and bring to the boil. Add the garlic, spring onion, ginger, salt and vinegar. Let it simmer for 2 minutes to start the flavours infusing, then add the chicken. Bring the water back up to a low simmer and put a lid on. Leave on a low simmer for 20 minutes, then turn off the heat and leave for a further 40 minutes, still with the lid on.

Once 40 minutes has passed, take the lid off and gently remove the chicken, making sure to pour out any liquid from inside its cavity and drain well. Leave the chook to rest and cool on a small tray. Leave the 'started' broth to sit until the chicken is cool enough to handle. Now is a good time to water the garden or listen to an album that goes for about half an hour.

When the chicken is cool and rested, pick off all the meat and store it in the fridge. You can use it for soups, sandwiches, anything. Return the bones and resting juices to the pan, turn the heat up high and bring up to a boil.

Set up a ladle and a bowl on the side of the stove. Skim any foamy and fatty bits off the top of the broth as it comes up to boil. Repeat this process regularly, about every 10 minutes for the first half an hour. Once the broth threatens to boil angrily, lower the heat so it simmers down. A few rolling bubbles here and there is a good heat.

After the first half an hour of simmering, most of the impurities should have come out of the broth and you can pop the lid back on. Keep simmering – the broth will be tasty and ready to eat after about 4 hours but to extract the maximum amount of nutrients the broth can cook for up to 24 hours. For extended cooks like this, it's important to leave the lid on to stop the broth evaporating.

Once the broth is cooked, turn off the heat and leave to cool to a safe temperature. Pour the broth through a fine sieve. Discard the bones and vegetables. Chicken broth will keep for about 5 days in the fridge or 3 months in the freezer.

CHICKEN SOUP WITH KALE & SWEETCORN

Chicken and corn soup is a comfort-food favourite, but this has more zing than the version you might remember from your childhood. I've added kale for both nutrition and flavour. The leafy green gets a lot of press these days for its health benefits, but the thing people forget to mention is that it's bloody delicious!

SERVES 4

2 litres (70 fl oz/8 cups) Chicken Broth (see opposite) or more or less depending on your appetite

½ bunch kale, thinly sliced, stalks and all

1 sweetcorn cob, kernels removed

1 carrot, thinly shredded

1 small zucchini (courgette), thinly shredded

1 teaspoon raw (demerara) sugar

3 tablespoons fish sauce (or to taste)

meat from ½ poached chicken (or thereabouts), see opposite

coriander (cilantro) leaves, to serve

Fermented Chilli Paste (see page 48), to serve, optional

Bring the broth to a boil in a large saucepan over medium heat and add the vegetables. Leave to simmer for about 5 minutes then turn off the heat. Add the sugar and fish sauce to taste.

Place equal amounts of poached chicken into your favourite serving bowls. Divide the hot broth and vegetable mix equally among the bowls. The broth will be hot enough to warm the chicken through. Chop some coriander and sprinkle over the top to serve (parsley or chives can be used instead if coriander isn't your bag). If you like, spoon in some fermented chilli paste for an extra flavour kick.

Any remaining soup will keep in the fridge for up to 4 days – a mug of the leftover soup is a great afternoon snack.

CHICKEN SOUP WITH KALE &
SWEETCORN (SEE PAGE 75)

BEEF SOUP WITH GREENS &
MUSHROOMS (SEE PAGE 79)

BEEF BROTH

A great base for soups and sauces, this flavour-packed beef broth is also an excellent source of nutrients. If you are short of time, you could get away with cooking the broth for 6–8 hours, but the longer the cooking time, the more nutrient-rich and delicious the broth will be.

MAKES ABOUT 4 LITRES (140 FL OZ/16 CUPS)

2 kg (4 lb 8 oz) beef bones
olive oil
2 brown onions, peeled
   and quartered
2 carrots, roughly chopped
   into 2 cm (¾ inch) chunks
2 celery stalks, roughly
   chopped into 2 cm
   (¾ inch) chunks
4 garlic cloves, peeled
   and smashed
30 ml (1 fl oz) apple cider
   vinegar, ideally with a live
   'mother' (see page 49)
1 teaspoon salt

Preheat the oven to 180°C (350°F). Place the beef bones in a roasting tin and cook for 30 minutes to render (melt away) the excess fat. Remove from the oven and drain the liquid fat into a glass jar. You can keep this in the fridge – it will last for months and is super tasty when used to roast vegetables.

Place a large saucepan or stockpot over high heat. Add a splash of oil, throw in the onions and stir. When the onions are beginning to brown after a couple of minutes, throw in the carrots. Fry the carrots for 2 minutes, then add the celery and garlic. Cook the vegetables for another 5 minutes, stirring often.

Add the bones, vinegar and 5 litres (175 fl oz/20 cups) of water, and bring to the boil. With a ladle, skim the fat and impurities that rise to the top. Turn down the heat to a low simmer. Ideally you want the broth to be cooking at around 80–90°C (175–195°F) to extract maximum vitamins, nutrients and flavour from the bones.

Leave uncovered for the first 30 minutes, skimming the top often, then cover with a lid and lower the heat slightly. Covering the broth will keep it a little hotter but also stop it from evaporating too much. Cook the broth for a minimum of 6–8 hours. This timeframe is enough to achieve a tasty broth, but overnight is optimal.

Once the broth is cooked, strain through a fine sieve and it's ready to go. There will still be some fat in it at this stage, which I like to leave, but if it's not to your liking, put the broth in a container in the fridge. As it cools down, the fat will rise to the top and set. It can then easily be removed and discarded. Beef broth will keep for about 1 week in the fridge and 3 months in the freezer.

NOTE: You can add beef brisket or shin to the broth to enhance the flavour. Roughly chop 400 g (14 oz) of meat and add it to the pan when the water starts to boil (you may need to ladle out some water so the pan doesn't overflow). Cook the beef for 2–3 hours until it's very tender, remove from the broth and refrigerate. Top up the pan with water and cook, covered, for another 4–6 hours. Slice the beef thinly when cold and use in sandwiches, soups and salads.

BEEF SOUP WITH GREENS & MUSHROOMS

Braised beef is great here but you can also thinly slice some steaks – sirloin, fillet and rump are perfect cuts for the occasion. If you feel up to it, thinly sliced beef heart is also awesome to use on its own or along with the other beef.

SERVES 4

2 litres (70 fl oz/8 cups) Beef Broth (see opposite) or more or less depending on your appetite
½ bunch leafy greens (kale, silverbeet/Swiss chard, whatever you have in the fridge), finely chopped
8 Swiss brown mushrooms, thinly sliced
2 spring onions (scallions), thinly sliced
1 teaspoon salt
400 g (14 oz) beef (braised or raw, depending on preference), thinly sliced
Fermented Chilli Paste (see page 48), to serve, optional

NOTE: *Beef-cut names can be troublesome. Sirloin (in Australia and the UK) is also known as short loin (in the US); the eye fillet (Australia) is also called the tenderloin (US); and the rump (Australia) is known as the round (US).*

Pour the broth into a saucepan over high heat and bring to the boil. Add the vegetables and let them simmer gently for 3 minutes. Season the broth with salt to taste – I suggest about 1 teaspoon.

Place the braised or raw beef in your serving bowls and pour over the hot broth and vegetable mix. The broth will be hot enough to warm the braised beef or lightly cook the raw beef. If you like, spoon in some fermented chilli paste for an extra flavour kick.

Serve. Eat. Enjoy.

FISH BROTH

White-fish bones are the best for a nicely balanced broth. Snapper, whiting or West Australian dhufish bones, say. Big-flavoured fish, such as salmon or kingfish, will obviously make a big-flavoured broth. Fish heads and wings are excellent to use in addition to the skeletal frame.

If your fennel comes with the frondy tops attached, they're perfect to use in the broth, and you can save the simmered bulb for a soup or salad afterwards. The whole fishy concoction is an excellent source of iodine, calcium, glycine, proline and phosphorus.

MAKES ABOUT 4 LITRES (140 FL OZ/16 CUPS)

1 kg (2 lb 4 oz) fish bones
2 brown onions, peeled and quartered
2 celery stalks, roughly chopped into 2 cm (¾ inch) pieces
½ fennel bulb, tough outer layer removed, roughly chopped into 2 cm (¾ inch) pieces
4 garlic cloves, peeled and smashed
5 cm (2 inch) piece ginger, scrubbed and sliced
30 ml (1 fl oz) apple cider vinegar, ideally with a live 'mother' (see page 49)

Wash the fish bones under cold running water to get rid of any blood and guts. Place in a large saucepan or stockpot once thoroughly clean. Add the vegetables, garlic and ginger to the pan. Fill with 4 litres (140 fl oz/16 cups) of water and place over high heat. Add the vinegar and bring to just under the boil. Lower the heat to a light simmer and skim away any impurities with a ladle. Continue skimming often for the first 10 minutes. Place a lid on the pan and lower the heat slightly.

Cook the fish broth for 4 hours. Once ready, strain through a fine sieve.

Fish broth will keep for about 3 days in the fridge and 3 months in the freezer.

FISH SOUP WITH MUSSELS & TOMATO

This is exactly the kind of dish you want to put on the backyard table when the sun's out and tomatoes are at their best.

SERVES 4

1 kg (2 lb 4 oz) mussels
2 litres (70 fl oz/8 cups) Fish Broth (see opposite)
1½ tablespoons vegetable oil
2 tomatoes, chopped into 1 cm (½ inch) chunks
1 red capsicum (pepper), chopped into 1 cm (½ inch) chunks
½ fennel bulb, tough outer layer removed, chopped into 1 cm (½ inch) chunks
2 garlic cloves, thinly sliced
150 ml (5 fl oz) white wine
1 handful flat-leaf (Italian) parsley, chopped

Scrub the mussels and remove the hairy beardy bits. Discard any broken mussels, or open ones that don't close when tapped on the bench. Rinse well.

Pour the broth into a large saucepan or stockpot and place over high heat. Bring to just under a boil, turn off the heat and let the broth sit.

Place another large saucepan over high heat. Once the empty pan is smoking hot, add a small splash of oil. Add the mussels and stir for about 30 seconds. Add the vegetables, garlic and white wine. Once the wine has boiled, place the lid on the pan and cook for 2 minutes. The mussels will start to pop open. Pour over the hot broth and bring to the boil. By this stage all of the mussels should be open and cooked (you can prise open any that remain closed; they will be fine to eat unless they smell bad).

Taste for seasoning – mussels are naturally salty so you might not need to add any extra salt. Ladle the mussels and broth into healthy-sized bowls and sprinkle generously with the parsley.

Serve with crusty bread and a big glass of rosé.

FISH SOUP WITH MUSSELS
3 TOMATO (SEE PAGE 83)

VEGETABLE SOUP WITH
ASIAN FLAVOURS (SEE PAGE 87)

VEGETABLE BROTH

This wonderful soup base is a great way to use up any old vegetable scraps and turn them into a delicious meal that won't break the bank.

olive oil
2 brown onions, peeled and quartered
2 carrots, chopped into 2 cm (¾ inch) chunks
2 celery stalks, chopped into 2 cm (¾ inch) chunks
2 tomatoes, chopped into 2 cm (¾ inch) chunks
1 leek, pale part only, chopped into 2 cm (¾ inch) chunks
½ fennel bulb, tough outer layer removed, chopped into 2 cm (¾ inch) chunks
4 garlic cloves, peeled and smashed
5 cm (2 inch) piece ginger, scrubbed and thinly sliced
2 pieces kelp, roughly 20 cm (8 inches) long
10 black peppercorns
30 ml (1 fl oz) apple cider vinegar, ideally with a live 'mother' (see page 49)
6 thyme sprigs
6 flat-leaf (Italian) parsley stalks (optional)

Place a stockpot over high heat and add a splash of olive oil. Add the onion and cook for 3 minutes until it starts to brown. Add the other vegetables and fry over high heat for 5 minutes, stirring often. Add the garlic, ginger, kelp, peppercorns and vinegar. Stir through and add 6 litres (210 fl oz/24 cups) of water and the fresh herbs. Bring to just under a boil.

Lower the heat until the broth is lightly simmering and skim off any impurities with a ladle. The vegetable broth needs to cook for 2 hours uncovered – it's good to let this broth reduce a little to enhance the flavour. Once cooked, strain through a fine sieve.

Vegetable broth will keep for about 1 week in the fridge and 3 months in the freezer.

NOTE: *Kelp can be found on beaches all over Australia (check with local councils for any harvesting rules). If you can't find fresh kelp, most Asian grocers and some health food stores have the dried variety. Make sure you soak the kelp in fresh water for at least 4 hours (and preferably overnight) before using to extract some of the salt.*

VEGETABLE SOUP WITH ASIAN FLAVOURS

Any of your favourite vegetables and pantry staples can be added to vegetable broth for one of the healthiest meals possible. Here I've gone with Asian flavours: kimchi, soy and coriander (cilantro).

SERVES 4

2 litres (70 fl oz/8 cups) Vegetable Broth (see opposite) or more or less depending on your appetite

2 cups mixed diced vegetables, such as carrots and celery

½ bunch leafy greens, such as kale and silverbeet (Swiss chard), finely chopped

370 g (13 oz/2 cups) cooked brown rice

200 g (7 oz/1 cup) Kimchi (see page 63)

2 hard-boiled eggs

2 tablespoons soy sauce

coriander (cilantro) sprigs, to serve (optional)

Pour the broth into a large saucepan and place over medium heat. Bring the broth to just under a boil. Add the diced vegetables and lower the heat to a simmer. Cook for 2 minutes, then add the greens.

While the broth simmers away, divide the rice and kimchi among four serving bowls. Cut the eggs in half and place in the bowls, too.

Add the soy sauce to the broth and taste – if you think it needs more salt, add a little more soy. Pour the broth and vegetable mix into your serving bowls with the rice and kimchi. Finish with coriander, if using. Feel invigorated.

SEAWEED BROTH

Seaweed is the fastest growing plant in the world so it's extremely sustainable and we should be consuming more of it. Kelp washes up on beaches all over Australia. It's easy to find, nutritious and extremely tasty, being naturally high in umami.

Once you've (legally) foraged your kelp, soak it in fresh water for at least 4 hours and preferably overnight. This will extract some of the salt so it's not too strongly flavoured.

This broth is a great base for a soup or a simple sauce for a noodle dish.

MAKES ABOUT 4 LITRES (140 FL OZ/16 CUPS)

300 g (10½ oz) fresh kelp,
   or 100 g (3½ oz) dried
2 carrots, chopped into 2 cm
   (¾ inch) chunks
5 cm (2 inch) piece ginger,
   thinly sliced
4 garlic cloves, peeled
   and smashed
4 spring onions (scallions),
   chopped into 2 cm
   (¾ inch) pieces
2 tablespoons miso paste
30 ml (1 fl oz) apple cider
   vinegar, ideally with a live
   'mother' (see page 49)

NOTE: *Check with the local council for any rules about harvesting kelp. If you can't find fresh kelp, most Asian grocers and some health food stores have the dried variety.*

Combine 5 litres (175 fl oz/20 cups) of water with all the ingredients in a large saucepan or stockpot. Place over high heat and bring to just under a boil, then turn down the heat to a light simmer. Skim off any impurities and cook for 2 hours. Strain through a fine sieve.

Seaweed broth will keep for about 10 days in the fridge and 3 months in the freezer.

CHILLED GREEN BROTH

The avocado is the star here; its buttery, grassy character bolstered by the other ingredients. This makes enough for a small cup of soup per person.

SERVES 4

1 green chilli
2 avocados, peeled and
  stones removed
1 garlic clove, peeled
  and smashed
3 Lebanese (short) cucumbers,
  roughly chopped
1 teaspoon mountain pepper
  leaf (or white pepper)
30 ml (1 fl oz) apple cider
  vinegar, ideally with a live
  'mother' (see page 49)
800 ml (28 fl oz) Seaweed
  Broth (see opposite)
1 teaspoon salt

Remove the stem of the green chilli, cut lengthways and remove the seeds. Mix together with the avocado, garlic, cucumber and mountain pepper leaf. Place half of this mix into your blender and purée until smooth.

Add half the vinegar and half the seaweed broth. Blend again. Pour this mixture into a large jug. Repeat this process with the remaining ingredients. Mix both batches together and season with the salt. Refrigerate for at least 2 hours so the broth is cold before serving.

Chilled green broth will only last about 2 days in the fridge and is best eaten on the day it's made.

NOTE: *Mountain pepper leaf can be bought from online bush food and herb and spice specialists.*

GREEN GAZPACHO

Turning the chilled green broth into a healthy, filling meal is a breeze.

SERVES 4

120 g (4¼ oz) stale bread
extra virgin olive oil
2 quantities Chilled Green
  Broth (above)
1 iceberg lettuce, quartered
1 Lebanese (short) cucumber,
  roughly cut into 8 chunks
2 spring onions (scallions),
  thinly sliced
100 g (3½ oz) feta cheese
1 large handful coriander
  (cilantro), flat-leaf (Italian)
  parsley and mint leaves

Roughly tear up the bread and cook in a little oil in a frying pan over medium heat to slightly crisp it.

Pour the broth into four bowls and place a lettuce chunk in the centre of the broth. Divide the cucumber, spring onion and fried bread between the bowls and crumble over some feta (any other cheese can be used if you're not a feta fan). Finish with the mixed herbs and a drizzle of olive oil.

CHILLED GREEN BROTH (SEE PAGE 89)

GREEN GAZPACHO (SEE PAGE 89)

DRIED & POWDERED

I love to dry and powder ingredients that might otherwise end up in waste. They keep for ages, have the most vibrant colours, and add instant pizzazz to anything. If you don't own a dehydrator, you can pick up a basic model pretty cheaply these days from most major department and cookware stores. Alternatively, you can always use your oven on a very low heat.

ORANGE SKIN

A little bit of this dusted over meringue or chocolate cake makes a big impression, but don't be afraid to experiment with it on shellfish (such as yabbies or bugs), or even duck in a twist on duck à l'orange.

When you're juicing oranges, peel the orange skin off with a vegetable peeler. A little bit of white peel is okay, but not too much. Dry in the dehydrator or in an oven at 55°C (130°F) for 7–8 hours until crisp. Leave to cool and then blend to a fine powder.

HERBS

We grow lots of herbs at home and it's rare we ever get through them all. Instead we pick the extras and turn them into vibrant, flavourful powders. I like to use mint, lemon balm, flat-leaf (Italian) parsley stalks and coriander (cilantro) leaves, stalks and seeds.

Pick, wash and dry your herbs. Dry in the dehydrator or in an oven at 45°C (115°F) for 5–8 hours, depending on how long the herb takes to become brittle. Leave to cool, then give them a crush and grind to a fine powder. Pass the powder through a tea strainer to remove any woody bits.

How you choose to use the powdered herbs depends on the flavour combination you've created. A combination of mint and parsley, for example, would work sprinkled over a pea soup, while powdered nasturtium gives zing to chocolate pudding. As always, experiment and enjoy.

SPRING ONIONS

There's so much flavour in the green tops of spring onions (scallions). We always have a bunch in the fridge and Mum always has a whole bed of them growing at home when they're in season.

Dry the tops in the dehydrator or in an oven at 60°C (140°F) for about 10 hours until brittle. Leave to cool, then give them a crush and grind to a fine powder. Pass the powder through a tea strainer. You will end up with a bright green flavourful ingredient.

Spring onion powder is amazing with noodles and chilli, sprinkled over potato salad or with grilled cheese on toast.

YOGHURT

Dried yoghurt can be served with lots of cheerful summer berries for a beautiful, simple and delicious dessert. Line a tray with baking paper and spread plain yoghurt thinly on top. Dry in the dehydrator or in an oven at 65°C (150°F) for 8–10 hours. Break into shards or blend into a powder. Don't grind this one – it's better with a bit of texture.

PASSIONFRUIT

When making Passionfruit Tarts (see page 178), you will be left with the fruit's skins and seeds. These have a great aroma when dried and powdered.

Chop the skins into quarters. Dry in a dehydrator or in an oven at 55°C (130°F) for 20 hours (it's a long time, yeah, but those skins are tough buggers). Add the seeds at the 12-hour mark. When dried, blend the skins and seeds and pass through a tea strainer.

Most desserts benefit from a dusting of passionfruit powder every now and again (g'day, pavlova) but this is also a nice way to jolt your morning fruit and yoghurt to life.

KELP

I always have dried kelp powder in my kitchen, both at work and home. It's a massive flavour booster – I like to think of it as nature's MSG.

Wash the kelp well to remove all the sand before you do anything. It can just hang in a dry warm place for a few weeks to air-dry but if you want to speed up the process, dry it in a dehydrator or an oven at 70–80°C (160–175°F) for about 8 hours until crisp. Crush it up with your hands, then place it in a spice grinder and blend to a fine powder. Pass through a tea strainer, store in a jar and sprinkle on roasted meats, vegetables and salads for an incredible seasoning hit.

ROSES

Be sure to source roses that are free from sprays. Note that the better they smell, the better they'll taste.

Pick the petals and lay them evenly on a dehydrator tray or baking tray. Dry in a dehydrator or in an oven at roughly 80°C (175°F) for 6–8 hours until crisp. Gently crush them between your fingers. I like the rose petals to be flaky. These are great sprinkled over desserts and used in Middle Eastern dishes. They'll keep well in a jar for a few months.

STRAWBERRIES

When strawberries are at their seasonal peak and lowest price, it's a great time to preserve that goodness in something other than jam (not that there's anything wrong with jam, mind). Dried strawberry chips are awesome to have in the pantry for desserts and breakfasts or just as a snack.

Wash the strawberries and leave them to dry. Cut off the top bit and slice the rest of the berry lengthways into roughly 3 mm (⅛ in) pieces. Arrange the sliced berries in a single layer on a tray lined with baking paper. Dry in a dehydrator or in an oven at 60°C (140°F) for about 10 hours until crisp. Store in a jar and they will keep for months.

4.
VEGETABLES

I love vegetables. There's nothing quite like the summer freshness of a new season tomato, the flavour burst of roasted beetroot (beet), or the wholesomeness of simply cooked greens.

And I love growing, harvesting and eating my own vegetables. I've learnt so much about food production in recent years from Joost, but also from Mum and Dad growing fruit, vegetables and herbs at home. We always had a good-sized vegetable patch when I was a kid and now it's bigger than ever. There is no better feeling than picking vegetables, warm from the sun, lighting the wood barbecue and cooking all afternoon.

My parents are lucky to have plenty of space and time to grow most of their own fresh produce and keep chickens for eggs. I now rent in inner-city Melbourne, and although we don't have a lot of space to grow food, we still manage to produce a fair bit of it. We have about 4 square metres of space in our garden bed, which used to be grass until one day my housemate and good mate Duncan and I decided it could be put to better use. And we've never looked back, with lots of lovely aromatic herbs constantly on the go and small seasonal crops of veggies such as tomatoes, cucumber, celery, radish, zucchini (courgettes), broad (fava) beans, peas, pumpkin (winter squash), eggplant (aubergine) and chilli.

Many of the dishes in this chapter can be the centrepiece of the table rather than just a side. There are so many different vegetables to put on the plate and so many delicious ways to prepare them. With such diversity on offer, I will often eat just vegetables for dinner four or five times a week. So, try some of these fail-safe dishes and techniques and share them with family and friends.

BEETROOT, STALKS & ALL

The beetroot (beet) is an incredibly versatile ingredient, especially when you use the whole plant. If you find nice, fresh, medium-sized beets, the leaves and stalks are great to use. They have a sweet earthy flavour, and can be used as you would kale or cabbage. This dish is also vegan, but you can add cheese or yoghurt as you wish when serving.

SERVES 4–6

10 medium-sized
   beetroot (beets)
250 ml (9 fl oz/1 cup) apple
   cider vinegar, ideally with
   a live 'mother' (see page 49)
110 g (3¾ oz/½ cup) raw
   (demerara) sugar
2 tablespoons salt
6 thyme sprigs
2 tablespoons fennel seeds
10 pepperberries
olive oil, for frying
1 brown onion, diced
2 garlic cloves,
   coarsely chopped
½ teaspoon ground cinnamon
½ teaspoon allspice
squeeze of lemon juice
extra virgin olive oil,
   for dressing

NOTE: *Pepperberries can be purchased online from bush food and herb and spice specialists.*

Remove the leaves and stalks of the beetroot and set aside. Soak the beetroot in water for about 15 minutes to make sure they're well washed. Use a mandolin to shave 2 beetroot into thin slices, then set these aside.

Place the remaining beetroot in a large saucepan and add the vinegar, sugar, salt, thyme, fennel seeds and pepperberries. Cover the beetroot with water and bring to the boil. Turn down to a low heat and simmer for 30 minutes. Test them with a small knife; if you can easily push the knife in, they're cooked. Turn off the heat and leave to cool in the liquid.

Wash the beetroot leaves and stalks in cold water. Discard any scrappy looking leaves but keep any small attractive ones to use as a garnish (set these aside). Cut the stalks from the leaves. Thinly slice the stalks and leaves but keep them separate.

Heat a large splash of olive oil in another large saucepan over medium heat. Add the onion and cook for 3 minutes, stirring often. Add the garlic and cook for 2 minutes. Add the cinnamon and allspice, stir well and cook for 1 minute. Add the sliced stalks, stir and cook for about 5 minutes. Add the chopped beetroot leaves and a pinch of salt and cook over low heat, stirring often, for 15 minutes.

While the leaves and stalks are braising, remove the beetroot from the cooking liquid. The skin should peel away easily. Cut them into random-sized chunks.

Check the beetroot leaves and stalks for seasoning once they're tender. I like to add a small squeeze of lemon juice, a dash of extra virgin olive oil and a little more salt. Serve the leaves and stalks on a large plate with the beets. Scatter some of the whole beetroot leaves and raw beetroot slices on top and serve.

CHARRED VEGETABLES, YOGHURT & SEEDS

This is a great dish for winter. Try to get same-sized root vegetables if possible. It's a fun one to cook because you get to burn everything. Charring the veg gives it a sweet smoky depth of flavour. You can use this method for any vegetables but I find root veg work well.

I like to make a big batch of the toasty, crunchy seed mix. It will keep in a jar for months and is a great way to liven up any salads or vegetables. Even something as simple as iceberg lettuce dressed with olive oil and heaps of this seed mix is a delicious side dish.

SERVES 8–10

4 carrots
4 turnips
4 beetroot (beets)
6 French shallots
4 parsnips
260 g (9¼ oz/1 cup) Yoghurt
    (see page 41)
juice of 1 lemon
extra virgin olive oil,
    for dressing
rocket (arugula) leaves,
    to serve
handful garlic flowers or
    garlic chives, finely chopped,
    to serve

TOASTED SEED MIX
155 g (5½ oz/1 cup) pepitas
    (pumpkin seeds)
145 g (5 oz/1 cup)
    sunflower seeds
55 g (2 oz/⅓ cup) chia seeds
50 g (1¾ oz/⅓ cup)
    nigella seeds
65 g (2¼ oz/⅓ cup) quinoa
50 g (1¾ oz/⅓ cup)
    sesame seeds

Get your wood-fired or gas barbecue cranking hot. Leave all the vegetables with their skins on. Place the whole vegetables on the grill. The idea is to really burn the outside of the veg, but you want to keep rolling everything around the grill so they cook evenly. This will take 10–15 minutes, depending on the vegetable.

As each vegetable becomes tender, remove it from the grill and place it on a tray (the shallots will cook first). Keep the tray covered – the steam will help to finish cooking the vegetables and keep them warm.

Once the vegetables are cool enough to handle, use a small knife to scrape off the burnt skins. A little charred piece here and there is fine. Chop the veg into random chunks and place into a mixing bowl. If you squeeze the shallots, the tender flesh should ooze out of the skins with ease. Set aside.

To make the toasted seed mix, toast the seeds one type at a time in a hot, dry frying pan over medium heat until they start to pop and smell toasty. Mix all the seeds together. You'll need about 40 g (1½ oz/¼ cup) of this seed mix for the vegetable salad. Store the rest in an airtight jar or container for another time.

Spread the yoghurt thickly on the base of a large serving plate. Dress the vegetables with a small squeeze of lemon juice, a drizzle of extra virgin olive oil and a pinch of salt. Randomly layer the vegetables on the yoghurt. Add a big sprinkle of the toasted seed mix and finish with a few rocket leaves and garlic flowers or chives.

CHICKPEA FALAFELS

These falafels are always a crowd pleaser. They're cheap to make and a top way to use up vegetable off-cuts and anything looking depressed in the bottom of the crisper. I like to use the tops of fennel and spring onions (scallions), flat-leaf (Italian) parsley and coriander (cilantro) stalks and old carrots. If you don't have anything lying around looking for a new lease on life, beetroot (beets) and carrots are great to use. You basically need enough puréed veg to lightly coat the chickpeas when mixed together.

The rice flour can easily be made by grinding uncooked brown rice to a fine powder with a spice grinder but can be replaced with any flour (I like to use a gluten-free flour to keep everyone happy).

MAKES ABOUT 20 FALAFELS

600 g (1 lb 5 oz/3 cups) dried chickpeas, soaked
300–400 g (10½–14 oz) vegetable off-cuts, washed and coarsely chopped
1 small onion, coarsely chopped
2 garlic cloves, coarsely chopped
3 teaspoons Baharat (see page 211)
2 teaspoons nigella seeds
1 teaspoon bicarbonate of soda (baking soda)
45 g (1½ oz/¼ cup) rice flour
1 lemon
vegetable oil, for frying
3 teaspoons salt
1 teaspoon sumac
Yoghurt (see page 41) and dill, to serve

NOTE: *The chickpeas need to be soaked for 2–5 days. Once they're covered with water just leave them in the fridge, though you may need to top up the water as they soak.*

Drain the chickpeas and place in a large mixing bowl. Place the vegetable off-cuts, onion and garlic in a food processor and blend until reasonably fine (it will get blended again so a few chunky bits are no drama). Using a spatula, scrape the vegetable purée onto the chickpeas and mix well.

You now need to blend the chickpea mixture. You might need to do this in a few batches. Loosely fill a food processor with the chickpea mixture and blend on high for 30 seconds. Open, scrape the mixture from the side and mix back in. It needs to be as smooth as possible, so place the lid back on and repeat this twice more. A few random chunks are okay but not too many. Once the mixture is smooth, return it to the mixing bowl. Add the baharat, nigella seeds, bicarbonate of soda and flour. Zest in the lemon rind (don't throw the lemon away!) and mix well.

If you own a deep-fryer, now is the perfect time to bust it out. If not, heat the vegetable oil in a large saucepan or stockpot until 180°C (350°F). The oil will need to be at least 5 cm (2 inches) deep.

Use your hands to roll the falafel mixture into balls about the size of a golf ball. I like to roll the balls into an oval shape but round is fine, too. Whatever tickles your fancy. In a few batches, carefully fry the falafels for 3–4 minutes until nicely browned. Remove from the oil, drain well and place in a bowl lined with paper towel. Season with the salt and sumac.

The falafels are awesome to eat while they're hot, but still great at room temperature. Serve with yoghurt for dipping, a sprinkling of dill and a few chunks of that lemon that you zested earlier.

SMOKY EGGPLANT DIP

With its deep, smoky flavour, this is the ultimate dip for me. It's best to cook the eggplants on a wood fire, but they also come up great cooked on the stovetop, straight on the flame (a word to the wise: keep the smoke away from the fire alarm). It's perfect with Barbecue Bread (see page 26) but also awesome with roasted lamb, oily fish or in a sandwich.

SERVES 6–8

2 medium-sized eggplants
  (aubergines)
4 garlic cloves, unpeeled
olive oil, for dressing
2 tablespoons tahini
2 tablespoons lemon juice
1 tablespoon raw honey
2 pinches of allspice
Yoghurt (see page 41) and
  sumac, to serve

Preheat the oven to 180°C (350°F).

Make sure the eggplants are at room temperature and not cold from the fridge so they cook more evenly. Cook the eggplants over an open flame. You want them to char and smoke (basically burn the hell out of 'em). Cook them until they're tender but still holding their shape, then transfer to a bowl and cover. Try and catch a bit of the smoke in with the eggplants if you can. They'll steam and smoke for a bit to finish the cooking. Leave to cool.

Dress the garlic cloves in olive oil and a pinch of salt. Roast in a small ovenproof frying pan in the oven for 10 minutes. If you're lucky enough to have a wood-fired barbecue going, you could throw a whole bulb of garlic into the ashes instead and let it cook slowly. When ready, peel off the 4 cloves needed for this dish.

Cut the tops off the eggplants and discard. Chop the eggplants into pieces and throw them into a blender, blistered skin and all. Blend to a fine purée. Squeeze the garlic cloves from their skins, and add them to the blender. Add the tahini, lemon juice, honey and allspice. Give everything a whizz and season with salt.

Serve with a scoop of yoghurt in the middle and a sprinkle of sumac. Dig in. Like I said, it's the ultimate dip.

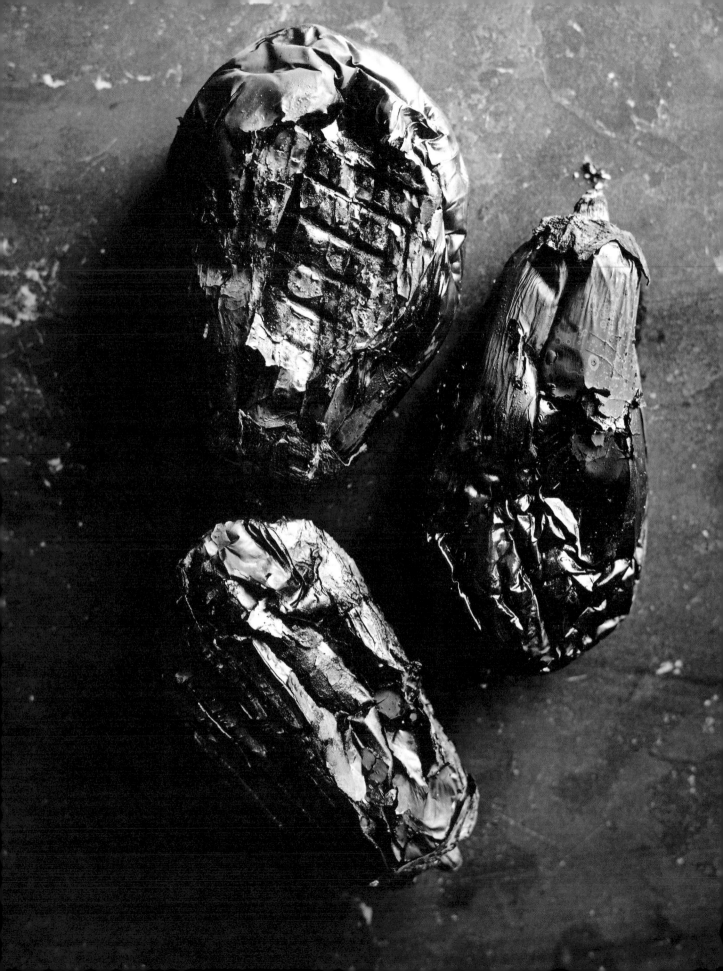

SMOKY EGGPLANT DIP
(SEE PAGE 105)

FERMENTED BROWN RICE, PEAS & ZUCCHINI

Okay, so this dish does take a long time, but it's totally worth it as the 'nutritious and delicious' factor is high. I like to use hand-harvested rain-fed rice. It's produced in a similar way to wheat so the fields aren't flooded to harvest or irrigated. The rice has a gnarly husk on it, the fibre and nutrient count is much higher than white rice, and its flavour is second to none.

SERVES 4

2 litres (70 fl oz/8 cups)
  Vegetable Broth
  (see page 86)
2 tablespoons olive oil
3 tablespoons butter
2 brown onions, finely chopped
2 garlic cloves, finely chopped
400 g (14 oz) medium-grain
  brown rice (see Fermented
  Grains, page 51)
180 g (6½ oz) zucchini
  (courgettes)
125 g (4½ oz)
  parmesan cheese
310 g (11 oz/2 cups)
  shelled peas
juice of ½ lemon
1 teaspoon spring onion
  powder (see Dried &
  Powdered, page 93),
  optional
1 teaspoon mint powder
(see Dried & Powdered,
  page 93), optional

Pour the broth into a medium saucepan and place over medium heat. When the broth is just under the boil, lower the heat and leave to simmer.

Put a large heavy-based saucepan over medium heat and add the olive oil and 2 tablespoons of the butter. Add the onion and cook for about 10 minutes, then add the garlic. Cook for a further 10 minutes until caramelised and sweet, and the smell is starting to make you feel quite hungry. This stage is very important as it's building the base of flavour for the whole dish. Keep a close eye on the onions and garlic so they don't burn.

Drain the fermented rice and add to the pan. Stir continuously for 3 minutes, then add the hot broth. Bring to a rolling boil and cook for about 20 minutes, stirring occasionally. While the rice is cooking, shave the zucchini into 3 mm (⅛ inch) rounds on a mandolin.

At this point, when the broth starts reducing and thickening, it will need another 10 minutes. It can't be left to its own devices and will need to be stirred continuously for the last stage of cooking.

When the rice is cooked and has a nice, smooth consistency, add the zucchini, cheese and peas, and stir through. Add the remaining tablespoon of butter, the lemon juice and a pinch of salt.

Serve with a generous and attractive dusting of the spring onion and mint powders, if using.

ROASTED PUMPKIN, SPROUTED LENTILS & TAHINI YOGHURT

This dish is great paired with slow-cooked lamb, but can easily be made the star of the table, too. Note that sprouted grains and legumes are considered super foods, but they come at a super cost. You pay about a tenth of the price by sprouting them yourself, and you can trace the provenance of the lentils to ensure you're buying locally grown. If you do choose DIY sprouts, you will need 3–4 days growing time, so plan ahead.

SERVES 4

1 butternut pumpkin (squash), about 600–700 g (1 lb 5 oz–1 lb 9 oz)
olive oil, for drizzling
4 tablespoons Baharat (see page 211)
3 tablespoons Tahini Yoghurt (see page 225)
1 handful flat-leaf (Italian) parsley leaves
1 handful coriander (cilantro) leaves
3 tablespoons Toasted Seed Mix (see page 103)
1 handful Sprouted Lentils (see below)

SPROUTED LENTILS
105 g (3½ oz/½ cup) French (puy) lentils
500 ml (17 fl oz/2 cups) water

If sprouting your own lentils, soak them in water in a jar covered with muslin (cheesecloth) or a tea towel (dish towel) secured with a rubber band. Leave on the kitchen bench overnight. Drain and rinse the lentils under cold water. Drain well and return to the jar. Cover with water and muslin as above and leave overnight. Repeat this process for 3 days. They should have sprouted after 3 days, but if not, leave for one more day. The sprouts will keep for 1 week in the fridge.

When you're ready to prepare the rest of the dish, preheat the oven to 200°C (400°F).

Halve the pumpkin and remove the seeds. Cut the flesh into half-moon-shaped wedges, about 3 cm (1¼ inches) thick, leaving the skin on. Place in a roasting tin and generously drizzle with olive oil. Sprinkle over the baharat spice and some salt. Mix really well with your hands so all the pumpkin is coated with oil and spice.

Spread the pumpkin slices evenly in the tin and place into the oven. Cook for about 10 minutes until the pumpkin has started to caramelise. Take out and turn the pumpkin. Cook until golden brown, for a further 10–15 minutes. If the pumpkin still isn't tender, lower the heat to 150°C (300°F) and cook until soft. If you prefer, the pumpkin can be grilled on the barbecue.

Place the pumpkin on a serving plate. Drizzle with the tahini yoghurt, sprinkle over the herbs, seed mix and sprouted lentils. Serve warm or at room temperature.

ROASTED BROCCOLI, ANCIENT BARLEY & ALMOND SALAD

Broccoli is a fantastic vegetable for roasting, and mixing it with barley makes the heartiest of hearty salads. By all means use normal barley if you don't have any of the fermented stuff on the go.

SERVES 4

150 g (5½ oz) fermented ancient barley (see Fermented Grains, page 51)
4 large red chillies
4 coriander (cilantro) roots with about 5 cm (2 inches) of stalk attached
1 red onion
4 garlic cloves
160 g (5½ oz/1 cup) almonds, skin on
2 medium-sized broccoli heads
olive oil, for drizzling
Mixed Pepper (see page 211), for sprinkling
2 large handfuls flat-leaf (Italian) parsley, leaves picked and chopped
2 large handfuls coriander (cilantro), leaves picked and chopped
1 large handful mint, leaves picked and chopped
juice of ½ lemon, or to taste

Drain the barley and throw it in a large saucepan or stockpot with 1 litre (35 fl oz/4 cups) of water. Bring to the boil, then reduce the heat and cook for 30 minutes. Drain the barley and leave to cool.

Deseed the chillies (don't touch your face in the process, yeah?), wash the coriander roots and peel the onion and garlic. Give them all a good chop and pound to a rough paste using a mortar and pestle.

Preheat the oven to 220°C (425°F). Spread the almonds on a baking tray and lightly roast them for 5 minutes. Remove from the oven, chop and set aside.

Cut the broccoli into florets and roughly chop the nutrient-rich stalks. Combine the broccoli with the paste, drizzle with a generous splash of olive oil, and sprinkle on some salt and mixed pepper. Put this mixture in a roasting tin and cook for about 15 minutes. The paste needs to be caramelised and the broccoli just tender. Take the broccoli out of the oven and leave to cool slightly.

When the broccoli mixture has cooled, combine with the barley, almonds and herbs, and dress with a splash of olive oil, lemon juice and salt to taste. Serve at room temperature and feel instantly healthy.

ROASTED BROCCOLI, ANCIENT BARLEY
3 ALMOND SALAD (SEE PAGE 111)

PARSNIP & CAULIFLOWER SOUP WITH
BURNT BUTTER & CHEESE TOASTIES
(SEE PAGE 114)

PARSNIP & CAULIFLOWER SOUP WITH BURNT BUTTER & CHEESE TOASTIES

Nothing will warm you up quicker on a cold winter's day than a steaming bowl of parsnip and cauliflower soup. It's a perfect make-ahead meal to reheat for a snack or light lunch. Pair with a delicious cheese toasty and dinner is ready. Be sure to make extra toasties because one is never enough. But then I love grilled cheese!

SERVES 4

1 leek
2 tablespoons butter
1½ tablespoons olive oil
1 brown onion,
    coarsely chopped
2 garlic cloves, chopped
2 parsnips, coarsely chopped
2 litres (70 fl oz/8 cups)
    Chicken or Vegetable Broth
    (see pages 74 or 86)
1 medium-sized cauliflower

CHEESE TOASTIES
sourdough bread
wholegrain mustard
Fermented Cabbage
    (optional; see page 46)
grated cheese

BURNT BUTTER
100 g (3½ oz) butter
1 small handful sage leaves
    (about 20 leaves)
dash of balsamic vinegar

Cut the dark green top off the leek, put in the compost or discard (the light green bit is fine to use). Split the leek lengthways and give it a good wash – dirt loves to get inside those leeky layers. Cut into quarters lengthways, then cut into 1 cm (½ inch) dice.

Heat a heavy-based saucepan over medium–high heat, and add the butter and olive oil. Once the butter has melted, add the onion and cook for 2 minutes, stirring often. Add the leek and continue stirring for 2 minutes. Add the garlic, parsnips and a large pinch of salt and cook for another 5 minutes. Add 1.5 litres (52 fl oz/6 cups) of the broth and bring to the boil.

While you're waiting for the broth to come to the boil, remove the cauliflower florets from their core and cut them roughly into 2.5 cm (1 inch) pieces.

When the broth is boiling, turn the heat down and let it simmer for about 10 minutes. Add the cauliflower. The broth needs to be about 2 cm (¾ inch) above the vegetables. Add more broth if needed and bring back to the boil. Reduce the heat to a high simmer and cook for a further 10 minutes or until the vegetables are soft. Turn the heat off and let it sit for about 10 minutes to cool a little before blending.

A hand-held stick blender is good to use here (and saves on washing up) or you could use a standard blender and blitz the soup in a couple of batches. Whatever your choice of weapon, you'll need to blend the soup on a high speed for at least 1 minute until silky and smooth. Taste for seasoning and add more salt if needed.

Leave the blended soup on a low heat while you move on to the toasties and burnt butter.

To make the toasties, thickly slice your bread. Toast on one side under a hot grill (broiler). Once golden, take the bread out and flip over. Spread the uncooked side with some mustard and a thin layer of the fermented cabbage, if using. Cover liberally with grated cheese and grill until golden.

To make the burnt butter, bring the butter to the boil in a small saucepan over medium–high heat. Leave the butter bubbling and as it starts to brown, keep scraping the bottom of the saucepan so you mix in all the caramelising brown pieces of goodness. Once the butter is brown and your kitchen is smelling wonderfully nutty, throw in the sage leaves and stand back (they will hiss and spit a bit as they start to fry). Stir for 30 seconds. Stir in a dash of balsamic vinegar and cook for a further 30 seconds, then turn off the heat.

Serve the soup with a generous drizzle of burnt butter and some crispy sage leaves on top, and the cheese toasties on the side.

NOTE: *Any melting cheese that you have in the fridge is fine to use. I like sourdough but any bread is okay. Use Kimchi (see page 63) instead of fermented cabbage if you want an extra kick.*

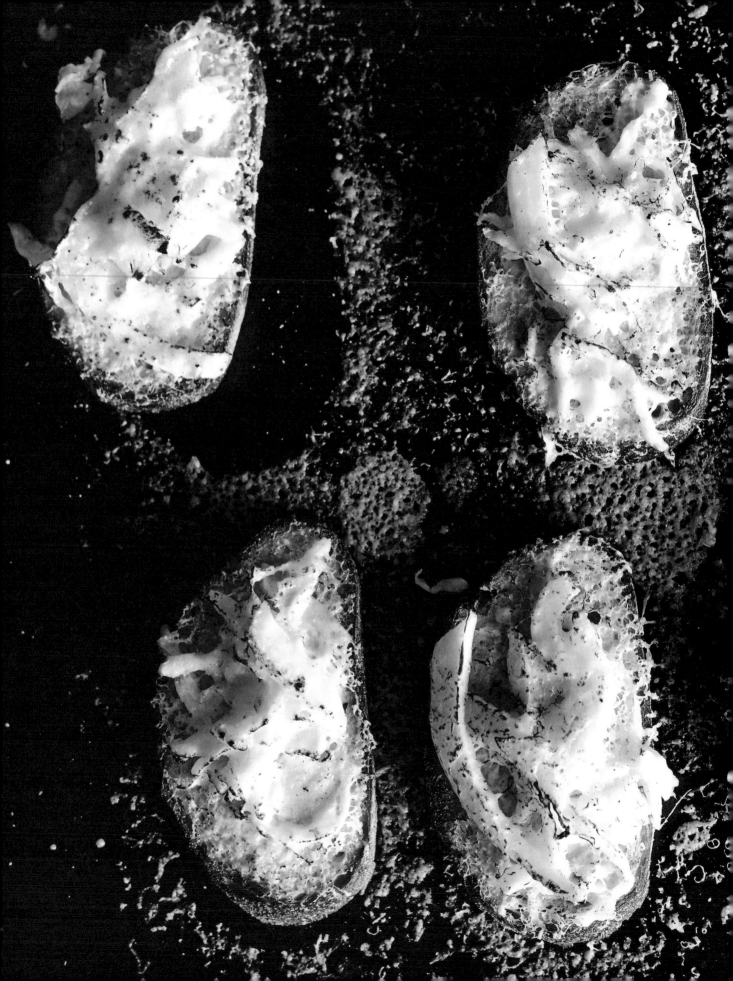

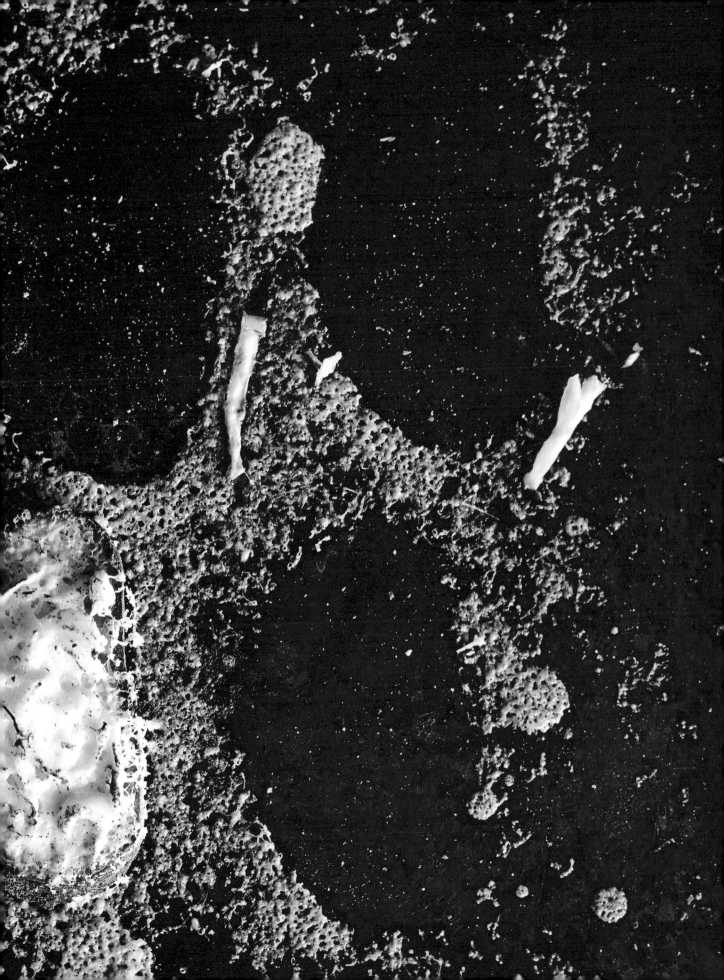

WITLOF, CITRUS, DATE & CORIANDER SALAD

This salad is fresh, zingy, healthy and so easy to make. There's an amazing balance of sweet, sour and bitter going on. Any citrus fruits can be used, whatever you have around. Mandarins, cumquats and limes will all work really well. It's the perfect side dish to a tagine or Moorish-style braised meats.

SERVES 4–6 AS A SIDE

2 oranges
2 blood oranges
1 pink grapefruit
2 finger limes (optional)
1 red witlof (chicory)
1 white witlof (chicory)
10 dates
1½ tablespoons olive oil
1 tablespoon powdered orange skin (see Dried & Powdered, page 93)
90 g (3¼ oz/1 bunch) coriander (cilantro), leaves picked

NOTE: *Finger limes are increasingly available in summer and autumn at farmers' markets and gourmet food stores, but can be bought frozen throughout the year from online bush food specialists.*

Peel the skins off the oranges and grapefruit with a vegetable peeler and set aside to dehydrate for next time. Cut the tops and bottoms off the oranges and grapefruit. Cut the remaining skin and white pith off the fruit, slicing from top to bottom and curving the knife as you cut to work with the shape off the flesh. Quarter the fruit and cut away any remaining white parts and seeds. Cut into roughly 2 cm (¾ inch) chunks and put in a mixing bowl. Halve the finger limes (if using) and squeeze out the little citrus pearls. Mix with the other fruit pieces.

Cut the bases from the witlof, about 1 cm (½ inch) from the bottom. Peel away the leaves. Once the leaves stop falling away, cut another centimetre of the stalk and continue peeling. Slice the large leaves in half lengthways and leave the smaller ones whole. Put into the mixing bowl.

Remove the seeds from the dates by pressing them between your fingers to squeeze each seed out. Tear the flesh into pieces and throw it in the mixing bowl.

Drizzle the salad with the olive oil and season with a pinch of salt. Mix together well.

Pick out the witlof leaves and place in a large shallow serving bowl. Pour the remaining citrus, dates and juice over the witlof. To finish, sprinkle over the powdered orange skin and scatter the coriander leaves on top.

QUINOA, TOMATO, RADISH & ZA'ATAR SALAD

Quinoa is so good!!! It's cheap and easy to prepare, and I eat it a few times a week. If you have some quinoa in the pantry, you can whip up a healthy meal or side dish in no time. Simply mix the cooked quinoa with anything that you have lying around. It can be as easy as adding some chopped herbs, nuts, dried currants, a splash of oil and a squeeze of lemon. Here the quinoa is jazzed up with fresh chopped tomatoes, peppery radishes and Middle Eastern spice mixes.

SERVES 4–6 AS A SIDE

200 g (7 oz/1 cup) quinoa
75 g (2¾ oz/1 bunch) flat-leaf
  (Italian) parsley
500 g (1 lb 2 oz)
  mixed tomatoes
12 radishes
1 tablespoon sumac
2 tablespoons Za'atar
  (see page 211)
3 tablespoons olive oil
1 tablespoon apple cider
  vinegar, ideally with a live
  'mother' (see page 49)

Half-fill a medium-sized saucepan with water and bring to the boil. Add the quinoa and cook for about 8 minutes or until tender. Once cooked, drain in a sieve, running a little cold water over the top to cool the quinoa down and stop it from overcooking. Leave to drain in the sieve for about 10 minutes.

Roughly chop the whole bunch of parsley – leaves and stalks. Randomly chop the tomatoes into chunks. Cut the radishes into quarters. Mix the quinoa, tomatoes, radishes and parsley in a bowl. Add the sumac, za'atar, olive oil, vinegar and a large pinch of salt. Mix thoroughly and serve.

SPINACH PANCAKES WITH HOT SAUCE & SOUR CREAM

This is a really quick recipe for breakfast, lunch or dinner. The spinach can be replaced with any leafy green and if you don't have any fresh herbs you can just use a few more greens.

SERVES 2

200 g (7 oz) English spinach
120 g (4¼ oz)
   self-raising flour
1 teaspoon baking powder
2 eggs, separated
150 ml (5 fl oz) milk
60 g (2¼ oz) butter, melted
½ teaspoon ground cumin
½ teaspoon ground coriander
1 very large handful
   flat-leaf (Italian)
   parsley, finely chopped
1 very large handful coriander
   (cilantro), finely chopped
4 spring onions (scallions),
   finely chopped
olive oil, for frying
   and dressing
mixed salad leaves, to serve
Sour Cream (see page 38)
   and Hot Sauce (see page
   221), to serve

Place a saucepan over medium heat. Add a splash of water and the spinach. Cook until just wilted and drain in a sieve. Once cool, squeeze as much water out of the spinach as possible and give it a rough chop.

To make the pancake batter, sift the flour and baking powder into a mixing bowl.

Add the egg yolks, the milk, butter, spices and a large pinch of salt. Mix until smooth. Add the spinach, herbs and spring onion and mix well. Whisk the egg whites until soft peaks form and carefully fold them in to the mixture.

Place a heavy-based frying pan over medium heat and add a splash of olive oil. Spoon in about 2 tablespoons of the batter and press down to a round pancake about 1 cm (½ inch) thick. Add as many as you can fit in the pan while still leaving some space between them. Cook for about 2 minutes until small bubbles start popping up, give them a flip and cook for another 2 minutes.

Once cooked, remove the pancakes from the pan, place on paper towel and cover with a tea towel (dish towel) to keep warm. Add a little more oil to the pan and continue cooking the pancakes until all the batter is used.

Dress the salad leaves with a little olive oil and season with salt. Serve the pancakes with dollops of sour cream and hot sauce on top and the fresh green salad on the side.

FRIED, SPICED CAULIFLOWER

I first cooked this dish for the opening party at the Greenhouse restaurant in Perth, and it's been on all my menus ever since. It's really easy to prepare and excellent with beer and a couple of mates.

SERVES 4

1 teaspoon ground cumin
1 teaspoon coriander seeds
½ teaspoon fennel seeds
½ teaspoon black peppercorns
2 teaspoons paprika
2 teaspoons salt
1 cauliflower
vegetable oil, for deep-frying

Toast the ground cumin, the coriander and fennel seeds, and the peppercorns in a dry frying pan over low–medium heat until fragrant. Wait for the mix to cool and then, using a mortar and pestle, grind it up along with the paprika and salt.

Remove the florets from the core of the cauliflower and cut them into roughly 2.5 cm (1 inch) pieces. Whip out the deep-fryer if you have one or heat a few centimetres of vegetable oil to 180°C (350°F) in a large saucepan. If you don't have a cooking thermometer, throw in a small piece of cauliflower – if it bubbles and fries straight away, the oil should be hot enough. Carefully place the cauliflower into the hot oil. Cook for a few minutes, stirring often, until golden in colour. Scoop out with a slotted spoon, draining off the oil, then dry on paper towel.

In a mixing bowl, combine the cauliflower with half the spice mixture. Serve with the remaining spice mixture on the side and crack open a beer.

ICEBERG, AVOCADO, CHILLI & FETA SALAD

Iceberg is possibly the most underrated lettuce ever. It's crunchy, juicy, cheap and lasts for ages when properly stored. This salad is quick and easy and is always a hit at barbecues.

There's no strict method to this salad. You're just chopping things and having a bit of fun, really.

SERVES 2

1 iceberg lettuce
1 large green chilli
1 avocado, peeled, stone removed and coarsely chopped
150 g (5½ oz) feta cheese, crumbled
6 spring onions (scallions), cut into small rounds
6 flat-leaf (Italian) parsley sprigs, leaves picked and chopped
4 oregano sprigs, leaves picked and chopped
80 ml (2½ fl oz/⅓ cup) olive oil
1 tablespoon apple cider vinegar, ideally with a live 'mother' (see page 49)

Smash the base of the lettuce on the bench and twist out the core. Remove any flappy outer leaves and cut the rest of the lettuce into random chunks. I like to leave the seeds in the chilli for this salad, so just give it a quick chop and you're good.

Toss everything together and dress with the oil and vinegar. Mix well. Serve. Done. Dusted.

GREENS, WEEDS & MYRTLE

This is a simple plate of greens and weeds, and it's great as a side to pretty much anything. Foraging is literally a walk in the park, by the way – check out pages 126–128 for info on how to do it.

Just grab a nice mix of whatever you can find – any weeds or beach herbs in Australia are good to use. In winter there are loads of mallow, dandelion and nasturtium leaves around the traps, and you should be able to find samphire, saltbush and barilla (dune spinach) on the coast most of the year. Have a look around where you live and get informed about the edible weeds in your area.

Two parts greens to one part weeds is a good ratio. If you're not able to find any weeds, the greens with the myrtle is still a killer combination.

SERVES 4 AS A SIDE

1 bunch kale or silverbeet
(Swiss chard), washed
½ bunch weeds, washed
2 tablespoons butter
1 teaspoon lemon myrtle
½ teaspoon aniseed myrtle
¼ teaspoon mangrove myrtle

NOTE: *If you can't track down aniseed or mangrove myrtle, substitute lemon myrtle instead. Most supermarkets stock lemon myrtle these days. Alternatively, you can buy myrtle online from herb and spice specialists.*

Pour 5 litres (175 fl oz/20 cups) of water into a large saucepan or stockpot, add a good pinch of salt and place over high heat.

Cut the stalks from the greens and chop the leaves into 10 cm (4 inch) pieces. The rougher the chop, the better. Pick all the stalks from the weeds (if you're using dandelion leaves, those guys should be fine to leave whole). Discard the stalks.

Once the water is at a rolling boil, add the greens and cook for 2 minutes. Add the weeds and bring it all back to the boil. Use a colander to strain the greens and weeds, and get as much water as you can out of them all by giving them a squeeze.

Return the empty pan back to the stovetop over high heat. Add the butter. Once the butter has melted, return the greens to the pan along with all the myrtle. Season with salt and mix well. Fry the greens for about 1 minute, stirring often.

Serve immediately and enjoy.

FORAGING

There is so much wonderful produce growing in the wild, waiting to be picked and enjoyed. The local park in Australia, for example, can be a goldmine of wild plants, such as native violet, chickweed, nasturtium and dandelion. Head to the coast and you can find beautiful edible succulents and warrigal greens.

WHY

There are so many reasons why I love to forage. There's the simple enjoyment of the environment, understanding the seasons, and eating plants in their most delicious and nutritious states. I encourage everyone to get outside and explore all the naturally growing food in your local environment. The rewards are many and splendid.

I love getting outdoors and picking food. I'd rather be outside with the sun shining than in a checkout line under fluorescent lights at a supermarket. It also becomes addictive. Once you pick up on a few of the common things around, you'll be spotting them everywhere. That's when it becomes really fun – just walking around and seeing what's in season and about to flower.

A lot of greens and weeds you can forage are really good for you, and if you're picking wild food, it's going to be at its freshest and most delicious. I also believe that if you pick your own food, you have a lot more respect and appreciation for it. You're less likely to forget about a bag of wild leaves in the back of the fridge if you picked them yourself. You'll also find yourself a lot more excited to bust them out and cook something amazing ...

HOW

Because it's such a trendy thing to forage, some people don't forage for the right reasons. They might do it because it's cool to put a wood sorrel (oxalis) leaf on your plate, even though it's not that relevant. However, foraging is much deeper than that. It's about respecting, understanding and immersing yourself in your environment.

A big motivation for me to forage is to gather food when it's in abundance, but I only pick what I need. In Melbourne, there is now a sign at St Kilda beach threatening that tree vandals will be prosecuted, because there were chefs heading down there and literally ripping out saltbush plants instead of taking a little bit here and a little bit there. Be respectful of the environment and leave an opportunity for the plant to regrow.

All my knowledge on foraging and wild food comes from handbooks on the subject. There are loads of guides out there on wild food, and I find the older and naffer a book looks, the better it's going to be, because it was written before foraging was cool. Just buy a little handbook covering your general area and before you know it you'll be spotting edible weeds everywhere. And it's easy! If you've picked a flower before, you can pick wild food. If you plan on taking home more than a handful, it's best to take a container and bag that you can carry your plants in so they won't get damaged.

Just a quick word on mushroom foraging. When it's the right season I love to spend a day in a creepy pine forest picking wild mushrooms. It's a real zen moment for a chef. Mushroom foraging, however, should be done with someone who is an expert in the field. It's tremendous fun, sure, but you want to be 100 per cent confident that what you're picking isn't poisonous. Luckily, with the popularity of foraging, you can now find individuals and groups on the internet offering guided forest picking trips when mushrooms are in season.

WHERE

The legality of foraging is different everywhere as local councils will have different conservation laws. In Western Australia, for example, dune conservation is a big thing so you can't just go traipsing through the dunes whenever you feel like it. Just check with the relevant authorities about guidelines for whatever park, strip of road or coastal area you're thinking about foraging in (taking plants from national parks, however, is a complete no-no, so don't even consider it).

When it is legal in a certain area, still be respectful of the seasons and environment. In peak summer, say, when conditions are harsh, don't even think about going to the coast to pick herbs. There might be plants there but they will already be struggling as it is.

There's so much opportunity to be found in your neighbourhood and front yard, too. On a walk around any suburb you can usually find lots of little edibles that are normally overlooked. Clover, dandelion, mallow, radish weed, wild radish and different types of wood sorrel (oxalis). So many bits and pieces.

There are wild brassicas, those small yellow flowers you see down the side of freeways on plants that look like broccoli leaves. The flowers have a cabbage-like, cauliflower taste, the leaves and stalks are great to ferment and the seed pods can be pickled.

A world of opportunity awaits when you discover the prevalence of wild foods and begin to understand how they change with the seasons.

COOKING

Wild weeds are delicious but they can also be quite strong when eaten raw, and might need some preparation to soften their astringency. This could be anything from a light braise to fermenting to drying and grinding into a powder. You should also give foraged ingredients a quick wash before using, particularly if they're picked from suburban areas.

Try and use wild ingredients not as a novelty, but as part of your day-to-day cooking. Instead of sautéing some kale, for example, you can throw in some mallow and dandelion. All of a sudden you've got different textures, different flavours and more nutrients. Beach herbs are a fantastic natural seasoning, too. Barilla (dune spinach) and saltbush have salt spray on them because they've grown in the wild near the coast with the winds blowing across them, so they add a lovely salty taste to a dish.

5.
SEAFOOD & MEAT

I'm a huge fan of using whatever produce is around me and is easily accessible. That could be a seasonal local fruit that's only available for a brief window during the year; a cheaper, less popular type of fish or cut of meat; or a bunch of ingredients at the back of the fridge that are about to reach their use-by dates.

I love to cook with native Australian fruits, greens and herbs but I also like to experiment with ingredients that many cooks wouldn't bother with – such as the cursed carp or foraged weeds. It's amazing what wonderful flavours and combinations can be achieved with a bit of imagination.

While many of the dishes in this chapter might seem unusual, they often reference a proven classic dish or technique that has been adapted using Australian ingredients. I take inspiration from countries with strong food cultures – Italy, China, France, Spain and many others. In English cuisine, it's common to match game meat with a tart fruit such as a cherry; in Australia we pair kangaroo with quandong. Making the most of local ingredients is a good idea wherever you live, as native produce is naturally better suited to the climate and growing conditions, and is usually a much more sustainable option than imported plants and animals.

Your local farmers' market is often the best place to source ethically produced, seasonal, local food – and shopping at them gives you the chance to meet and greet the people who intimately and expertly tend the earth for a living. The more you get to know the producers, the more respect you'll have for your food and the challenges farmers face. It also reinforces the importance of allowing the seasons to provide inspiration and direction in the kitchen.

It's easy to get carried away at a pumping market and buy too much. A good idea is to plan beforehand how many meals you're going to cook and then let the market inspire you. Also, take a few re-usable bags and a cooler bag with some ice bricks in summer to keep your meat and fish purchases nice and cold.

If markets aren't an option for you, try shopping at stores that source their produce locally. Look for fresh grass-fed meat and local organic options where possible. They shouldn't be too hard to find; organic shops are popping up all over the place. It'll make a big difference.

RAW SCALLOPS, NAM JIM & NUTS

This dish is a fantastic starter and a great way to use fresh scallops without the fear of overcooking them. I'd suggest serving this before a Thai curry, or with sashimi, oysters and pickled vegetables for a light summer dinner.

Sandalwood nuts are essentially a by-product of the sandalwood industry, and the trees are unique to Western Australia. The nuts are available online, and from some supermarkets and gourmet food stores (particularly in Western Australia). The nuts have a popcorny flavour and crazy texture – when you chew them, they almost turn into gum.

SERVES 2

8 large sashimi-grade scallops
Nam Jim Dressing (see
  page 220)
2 kaffir lime leaves
50 g (1¾ oz) sandalwood
  nuts, roasted and
  coarsely chopped
30 g (1 oz/¼ cup)
  bean sprouts
2 tablespoons store-bought
  fried shallots
6 coriander (cilantro) sprigs,
  coarsely chopped
2 tablespoons salmon or trout
  roe (optional)

NOTE: *If sandalwood nuts aren't available, you can replace with macadamia nuts, no worries.*

Slice the scallops crossways into thin rounds – you want about four slices from each scallop. Spread the scallops in one layer over a plate, covering most of the surface but leaving a little room around the edge. Generously cover with the nam jim dressing, which will slightly cure the scallops.

While the scallops are curing (for at least 10 minutes), remove the stems from the lime leaves and shred the leaves as thinly as possible lengthways. Scatter these over the scallops along with the nuts, bean sprouts, fried shallots and coriander. If using, add the salmon or trout roe here and there and serve at room temperature.

LAMB, CHICKPEA, POMEGRANATE & SAFFRON SALAD

This hearty salad has a lovely sour hit from the pomegranate, and floral notes from the saffron. I like to use lamb rumps with the fat caps attached, because they're far juicier and have a great flavour.

SERVES 4

400 g (14 oz/2 cups) dried chickpeas
4 red capsicums (peppers)
4 lamb rumps, about 600 g (1 lb 5 oz) in total
4 tablespoons Baharat (see page 211)
2 tablespoons salt
2 large handfuls flat-leaf (Italian) parsley leaves
1 pomegranate
Saffron Dressing (see page 226)
mint powder (see Dried & Powdered, page 93), optional

The chickpeas will need to be soaked in water overnight in the fridge. Drain the chickpeas from the soaking liquid, place in a medium saucepan and cover with cold water. Bring to the boil. Reduce the heat to just under a simmer and cook the chickpeas for about 45 minutes or until tender. Some white foam might rise to the top of the saucepan. Skim and discard it if it does. If the chickpeas rise above the level of the water, top things up with some fresh water. Once cooked, drain the chickpeas and set aside.

If you have a gas stove, turn the heat to high and place the capsicums over the flame. Using a pair of tongs to hold them, burn them on all sides. During this process they will cook and become tender. If you don't have a gas stove, you can grill the capsicums in a hot oven. Once they're nice and black, place them in a container and cover. The heat will steam off the skins and finish the cooking. Once cool enough to handle, peel off the skins and remove the stalks and seeds. Slice the capsicum cheeks into 1 cm (½ inch) thick strips.

Place a large frying pan over medium heat. Coat the lamb with the baharat and salt. Once the pan is hot, place the lamb in, fat side down. Cook for about 8 minutes to render the fat and caramelise. Once golden, turn and cook for another 8 minutes. I like the lamb to be cooked to medium. Turn off the heat and leave it to rest.

Place the chickpeas, peppers and parsley into a salad bowl. Cut the pomegranate in half and bash it with a wooden spoon over the salad bowl, cut side down. This will knock out the seeds and provide juice for the salad. Dress generously with saffron dressing.

Carve the lamb rumps into 2 cm (¾ in) thick slices and serve with the salad on a large platter. Sprinkle over some dried mint powder, if using, and eat immediately.

CHICKEN LIVER PARFAIT WITH RIBERRY SAUCE

Pâté is renowned for being bad for you because it has so much butter in it – and it's kind of true. But if you're using grass-fed butter and organic chicken liver it's not all bad, right? Especially if eaten in moderation, as liver is high in nutrients.

The pâté and riberry sauce are great mates as the riberry cuts through the pâté's richness. You can get frozen riberries easily from online bush food specialists, but you can substitute the riberries with cherries, no problem. There are a few steps in this recipe, but like any dish, the more you make it the easier it becomes. It's a proper crowd-pleaser and a stellar share-plate to make in advance if you're having guests over.

SERVES 6–8

PARFAIT
280 g (10 oz) chicken livers
milk, to soak
500 ml (17 fl oz/2 cups) port
2 French shallots,
    peeled and sliced
1 bay leaf
2 thyme sprigs
4 juniper berries
6 black peppercorns
310 g (11 oz) butter
2 eggs

RIBERRY SAUCE
125 g (4½ oz/1 cup)
    frozen riberries
55 g (2 oz/¼ cup) sugar
60 ml (2 fl oz/¼ cup) water
3 tablespoons olive oil
1 tablespoon lemon juice

NOTE: *A light-flavoured olive oil is best for the sauce.*

To make the parfait, trim any fatty white bits and connective sinew from the chicken livers. Place the livers in a bowl and cover with milk. The milk will help clean the livers and remove any extra blood that might be in them (it basically draws out the bitter flavour). They need to soak in the milk for at least 2 hours but overnight is better. Once they've had a good soak, strain the milk and discard. Rinse the livers under cold water and drain well, then set aside for about 30 minutes to bring to room temperature (if the livers are too cold, they will seize the butter when making the pâté).

Pour the port into a small saucepan and add the shallots, bay leaf, thyme, juniper berries and peppercorns. Place over high heat and bring to the boil. Reduce the port by half until it's thick and shiny. Strain the liquid, then leave to cool.

Preheat the oven to 160°C (320°F).

Dice the butter and place in a small saucepan over medium heat. You want the butter to be heated to about 35–40°C (95–105°F) – it should be runny but not bubbling. While the butter is melting, place the cleaned livers in your blender. Crack the eggs and add to the livers. Blend on high for a few minutes to make things as smooth as possible. Pour the liver mixture through a sieve into a tall jug, pressing through with the back of a ladle to make sure there are only the nasty, chewy bits left in the sieve.

From here you need to slowly pour the melted butter into the tall jug while blending with a hand-held stick blender to emulsify the butter and liver – just like you were making a mayonnaise. Mix in about half of the port reduction, some freshly cracked black pepper and a few pinches of salt. This is the challenging part of making this pâté.

Have a little taste of the mixture at this point. You should taste a little salt and the sweet aromatic flavour of the port. Adjust if needed – I like to slightly over-season as the flavour dulls when the pâté is cold.

Pour the mixture into a 22 x 12 x 6 cm (8¾ x 4¾ x 2½ inch) terrine mould or loaf (bar) tin. Place the mould into a deep roasting tin and pour some warm water into the tin – the water should come up to the level of the pâté in the mould. Cover with foil and place in the oven.

Check to see how it's going after 30 minutes. You want the pâté to have set and to wobble like a panna cotta. If you have a cooking thermometer, press it into the centre of the pâté – if it's between 55°C (130°F) and 60°C (140°F) it's ready to take out. Remove the pâté from the oven and lift the mould out of the water bath. Leave it to collect its thoughts on the bench for 30 minutes, then put it in the refrigerator. The pâté will keep for about a week in the fridge.

To make the riberry sauce, first place the riberries in a small saucepan with the sugar and water. Bring to the boil, then lower the heat and simmer for 10 minutes. Carefully pour the mixture into a blender and whizz to a fine purée. Slowly pour in the olive oil and lemon juice while it's blending. You should end up with a smooth and shiny sauce.

To serve, spoon out some of the pâté onto a plate or into a small bowl. Serve the riberry sauce on the side along with lavosh, toast or crackers.

HAY-SMOKED BEEF, ONIONS & MISO

This is the ultimate barbecue dish and a lot of fun to cook. The hay provides a lovely mellow smoky flavour and blackens the beef. Don't be afraid to give it a go — it's not that hard and really takes the flavour to another level.

SERVES 4

800 g (1 lb 12 oz) beef sirloin, in one piece
vegetable oil, for dressing
4 large handfuls hay
2 brown onions, skins left on and halved root to shoot
8 spring onions (scallions)
15 g (½ oz/¼ cup) store-bought fried shallots
1 medium handful flat-leaf (Italian) parsley, chopped
1½ tablespoons red miso
finely grated zest and juice of 1 orange
olive oil, for dressing
spring onion powder (see Dried & Powdered, page 93)

NOTE: *Sirloin (in Australia and the UK) is also known as short loin (in the US). The best place to buy hay in bales or small bags is your local pet store (I'm not joking!).*

Take the sirloin out of the fridge at least 30 minutes before cooking to come to room temperature. Season the beef generously with salt and dress with vegetable oil. Preheat the barbecue or get the wood fire going.

Place the beef on the hot barbecue chargrill plate or wood-fire grill and caramelise on all sides. This will take roughly 12–15 minutes of grilling time.

Throw a few handfuls of dry hay onto the beef to cover it completely (step back as the hay will catch fire quickly). Let the hay burn away and then repeat the process (this should take about 1½ minutes each time). Once the second round of hay has burnt away, remove the beef from the grill and let it rest. We want the beef to be rare.

While the beef is resting, dress the onions with a little oil and place cut side down on the grill. You want to burn the cut side. Once blackened, turn the onions and cook until tender. Remove the top third of the spring onions and keep for drying and powdering. Dress the remaining spring onion pieces with vegetable oil and throw them on the grill until they're charred and tender.

Once cooked, remove all the onions from the grill. Peel the brown onion skins and peel the layers apart into little cups. Roughly chop the spring onions into quarter lengths.

Place all the onions into a mixing bowl with the fried shallots, parsley and miso. Add the orange zest and juice, a splash of olive oil and a pinch of salt and pepper. Mix well. Return the beef to the grill to warm it through. Remove and slice thinly.

To serve, place a bit of the salad on the plate first, then a bit of the beef and then a bit more salad. Repeat this sequence a couple of times, then sprinkle with spring onion powder, to create the most awesome warm barbecue salad ever.

CHICKEN & GREEN MANGO SALAD WITH HOT & SOUR DRESSING

This salad sits on the sour side of the fence although I really love that. It's a bit Asian-fusiony, but mostly inspired by som tam, the Thai green papaya salad. I have so many fond memories of eating in Thailand, more often than not having my head blown off with extreme chilli heat. This reworking is a little tamer and more substantial with the addition of poached chicken.

SERVES 4

1 poached chicken (see Chicken Broth, page 74)
1 quantity Hot and Sour Dressing (see page 226)
2 tablespoons brown rice
2 green mangoes
2 Lebanese (short) cucumbers, halved lengthways, seeds removed, cut into angled slices 5 mm (¼ inch) thick
¼ Chinese cabbage (wong bok), sliced as thinly as possible
4 large red chillies
155 g (5½ oz/1 cup) cashew nuts
2 large handfuls coriander (cilantro) leaves
1 large handful mint leaves
1 large handful Thai basil leaves
230 g (8 oz/2 cups) bean sprouts

NOTE: *If you're running short of time, grab a barbecued chicken from the shops rather than poaching your own.*

Preheat the oven to 180°C (350°F).

Pull the skin from your poached chicken. I like to slice the skin thinly and use it in the salad, but leave it out if you prefer. Shred the chicken flesh into bite-sized pieces and place in your mixing bowl. Generously dress the chicken with hot and sour dressing. It will soak in and provide great flavour. Set aside.

Place the rice on a baking tray and toast in the oven for 8 minutes until golden brown. You can also do this in a dry frying pan over medium heat. Leave the rice to cool and then grind to a fine powder using a spice grinder or mortar and pestle.

Meanwhile, use a vegetable peeler to peel the mango and use a mandolin or sharp knife to slice it thinly. Lay the slices together and use a sharp knife to slice thinly into matchsticks.

Throw the sliced mango in with the chicken and combine. Mix in the cucumber and cabbage. Remove the stems of the chillies and slice in half lengthways. Remove the seeds and membrane and slice as thinly as possible top-to-bottom to get nice thin, long strips. Throw the chillies into the mix.

Toast your cashew nuts in a hot, dry frying pan until golden brown. Coarsely chop and mix in. Tear up the herbs and throw them into the salad, too. Add the bean sprouts and mix through. Add some more dressing if needed – it's good to have all the ingredients well coated and a puddle of dressing in the bottom of the bowl.

Serve in a large bowl and sprinkle over the rice powder. This salad is awesome with steamed rice on the side.

KANGAROO & AUSTRALIAN FRUITS, HERBS & SPICES

In my opinion, kangaroo is the most sustainable meat we can eat in Australia. It's estimated that there are three kangaroos to every one person in Australia and they are constantly being culled to prevent them from damaging farmland. Kangaroos eat natural wild food, not modified feeds, and are an extremely lean source of red meat. I think it's a no-brainer that we should be eating a lot more roo. I love to cook meats on a wood-fired grill or barbecue but a hot frying pan on the stovetop will also do the job.

The native fruits in this recipe bring a very acidic flavour to the dish and cut through both the gamey taste of the roo and the richness of the sauce. When preparing the quandongs, be sure to keep the seeds. Inside them is a small nut that has a beautiful marzipan flavour and these are great to infuse into milk or cream for a sauce or ice-cream base. If you're not likely to use them within a week or so, place them in the freezer and they'll keep for months.

SERVES 4

600 g (1 lb 5 oz) kangaroo loin
2 tablespoons Australian
   Seven Spice (see page 211)
6 quandongs
4 rosella (hibiscus) flowers
50 g (1¾ oz) riberries
50 g (1¾ oz) desert limes
50 g (1¾ oz) muntries
   (native cranberries)
400 g (14 oz) warrigal greens
1 large handful beach herbs
   such as saltbush, barilla
   (dune spinach), beach
   mustard and beach banana
250 ml (9 fl oz/1 cup) Beef
   Broth (see page 78)
vegetable oil, for cooking
2 tablespoons butter

Set yourself up well for this cook and it will all happen very quickly. Kangaroo loins will often be very clean when you purchase them from the butcher; however, if there is any visible sinew, trim it away with a sharp knife.

Place the roo loins in a bowl and add 1 tablespoon of the Australian seven spice and 1 tablespoon of salt. Mix well and leave on the bench to come to room temperature (about 1 hour should do it).

Meanwhile, make sure your native fruits are defrosted (unless you happened to score a fresh harvest, in which case, nice going). Run a small knife around each quandong and the seed should come out easily. Separate the rosella flowers into rosella petals. The other fruits are all good to leave whole.

Pick all the warrigal green leaves from their stems and wash well. Pick and wash all the beach herbs.

Place the beef broth in a smallish saucepan, leaving enough room to fit all the fruits. Place over medium heat and bring to a gentle simmer. Add the fruits and simmer for 2 minutes before taking off the heat and setting aside to infuse.

Place the kangaroo on a hot barbecue or grill, or in a frying pan with a dash of vegetable oil. Leave to caramelise for about 4 minutes, then turn. Cook for a further 4 minutes, depending on the thickness of the loins. I strongly encourage you to cook the kangaroo to rare but if that's not to your taste, medium will still be okay. Just be warned that if you start heading down the road to well done, the roo will become dry, chewy and almost inedible.

Take the kangaroo off the heat and leave to rest for the same amount of time that you cooked it.

While the roo is resting, put a large frying pan over medium heat and throw in the butter with a small splash of oil. Once the butter is melted and bubbling, add the warrigal greens. Cook for 3–5 minutes, stirring often, until the greens have wilted.

Throw the roo back on the heat to warm it up. Check your fruits to see how they're travelling. By this stage they should be nice and soft. If the broth has reduced too much, just add a splash of water to loosen it up.

Drain the greens of any extra liquid that has resulted from the cooking process. To really drain them well, place them in a tea towel (dish towel) and squeeze. The tea towel will also help keep the greens warm while you carve the roo.

Remove the roo from the heat and, on a 45-degree angle, slice it into 1 cm (½ inch) thick pieces. Place the greens on a warm serving plate and lay the roo on top. Spoon the cooked fruits onto the roo and pour over the remaining sauce. Sprinkle over the remaining Australian seven spice and about half a teaspoon of salt. Scatter over the beach herbs. Eat.

NOTE: *Australian fruits and greens can be bought online from specialist bush food sites. If the fruits are difficult to come by, fresh sour cherries, slightly unripe stone fruits or even citrus fruits will also do the job.*

KANGAROO 3 AUSTRALIAN FRUITS, HERBS 3 SPICES
(SEE PAGE 144)

MULLET, GRILLED COS, FINGER LIME, NASTURTIUM & ROE
(SEE PAGE 148)

MULLET, GRILLED COS, FINGER LIME, NASTURTIUM & ROE

I cooked this dish at a pop-up restaurant in Australia House in London for Tourism Australia. A chef from each state had a night to prepare a menu. Shannon Bennett did a night, Maggie Beer did a night, I did a night ... This was my main course. The organisers were a bit worried at first. Mullet has such a bad reputation for being a cheap, horrible fish. But it's delicious when prepared well. When it's nice and fresh, it's as good as anything else – and a quarter of the price. I said, 'Trust me. It's going to be fine' – and it was. Everyone loved it.

SERVES 4

2 whole sea mullets
  (or other small oily fish,
  about 1.2 kg/2 lb 10 oz
  in total)
1 tablespoon brown rice
2 baby cos (romaine) lettuces
2 finger limes
olive oil, for drizzling
2 tablespoons butter
juice of ½ lemon
2 tablespoons salmon roe
Nasturtium Sauce (see
  page 221)

NOTE: *Finger limes are increasingly available in summer and autumn at farmers' markets and gourmet food stores, but can be bought frozen throughout the year from online bush food specialists.*

Filleting your own fish is always best to ensure that it's fresh and at its best. If you don't feel up to it, I'd suggest choosing whole fish from the fishmonger and asking them to fillet it for you. Be sure to keep the bones to make a broth (see page 82). Make sure that the pin bones in the fish are removed (using tweezers is best for this). Also make sure that the rib bones are out of there.

Preheat the oven to 180°C (350°F).

Place the rice on a baking tray and toast in the oven for about 8 minutes until golden brown. You can also do this in a dry frying pan over medium heat and achieve a similar result. Leave the rice to cool and then grind to a fine powder using a spice grinder or a mortar and pestle.

Remove any large outer leaves from the cos lettuces and trim any brown bits from the base. Split the cos in half lengthways. Cut the finger limes in half lengthways too and, with a small knife, gently scrape the 'caviar' out. Set aside.

Season the fish with a good pinch of salt and lightly drizzle with olive oil before you place it in the pan. I like to cook fish skin side down, starting in a cold non-stick frying pan. Starting the fish in a cold pan makes it a very gentle cook and gives it a chance to render out some of the fat in the skin. I use this method for any oily fish. Place the cold pan over medium heat and add your fish fillets. As the pan starts to heat, the fish will begin to fry. You want to do most of the cooking on the skin side. Cook for about 6 minutes until the skin is golden and crisp. Gently flip the fish and cook on the flesh side for 1 minute. Remove the fish from the pan and set aside to rest.

Throw the butter into the frying pan and turn the heat up to high. Once the butter is melted and bubbling away, add the cos cut side down. You want to get some nice colour on them but don't cook them too much – you also want to retain some crunch. Once they are caramelised, squeeze in the lemon juice, leave for 30 seconds, then turn off the heat. Push the cos to the side of the pan, place the fish back in the pan to warm it up and dress it in the lemon and butter. Good times.

Be creative with the plating of this dish. You can plate it individually or as a share plate. I like to smear some nasturtium sauce on the plate, lay down a fish fillet and a cos heart, then mix the salmon roe with the finger lime caviar and scatter over willy-nilly. Sprinkle with ground brown rice, drizzle generously with olive oil and serve straight away.

OYSTERS, WHISKY & BACON

When it comes to oysters I'm normally a fan of eating them raw, maybe with a little citrus juice, but this dish is an exception. The oysters really need to be cooked on a barbecue chargrill plate or wood fire to achieve the best results. I first cooked these in Albany, Western Australia, on *Recipes that Rock*, the TV show I did with Alex James from Blur. I reckon Albany rock oysters are the best in the country. Alex and I trekked out to the oyster farm and helped with the harvest. I really wanted to do a dish with bivalve beauties but was stumped on exactly what to make as they taste so good natural. We had happened to visit a happy pig farm that afternoon, and were at a whisky distillery the day before, and thus the dish came together almost by itself. If you wanted to call it a modern take on oysters Kilpatrick, you wouldn't be far wrong.

SERVES 2–4

300 g (10½ oz) smoked belly bacon, finely diced into 3 mm (⅛ inch) cubes
90 ml (3 fl oz) whisky (probably don't use the good stuff)
juice of 1 lemon
1 dozen rock oysters, unshucked
few handfuls beach sand or rock salt

Preheat the barbecue or get the wood fire cranking so it's really hot.

Throw the bacon into a cold frying pan and place over medium heat. By starting the bacon in a cold pan it gives the fat a chance to render, meaning you won't need to add any oil. Stir the bacon often once it starts frying. Cook for about 8 minutes. Once the bacon is golden and crispy, add 70 ml (2¼ fl oz) of the whisky (be careful as it might flame if you're using some type of cask-strength rocket fuel). Once the whisky has reduced slightly, add half the lemon juice. Cook for a further minute, then turn off the heat.

Pop the oysters with a shucker but don't remove the lid. Place them on the grill, lid side up, and leave to cook for 5 minutes. The aim is to warm the oyster and let the flesh set slightly. Remove from the grill. Place the oyster in your hand on a tea towel (dish towel) to protect your palm from the heat and run a paring knife under the lid to cut the adductor muscle and remove the lid. Try and keep as much of the oyster juice in the shell as possible. The juice is what makes an oyster beautiful.

Spread a 2 cm (¾ inch) layer of beach sand or rock salt onto your serving plate. Press the oysters into the sand so they sit up nicely, being careful not to get any sand in the oyster as that would make for a very unpleasant eating experience. Spoon over the bacon and whisky mixture and drizzle each oyster with a few drops of the remaining whisky and lemon juice. Serve straight away, ideally with more whisky.

CLAMS, CIDER & HERBS

This is a very clean, light dish. Mussels can replace the clams but I find their flavour is a little stronger and not as sweet. A mix of barilla (dune spinach), saltbush, beach banana and sea parsley is great. If you can't get a mix of beach herbs, just one or two of them is okay, and if you can't get your hands on any, you can use chervil, chives or parsley instead.

SERVES 4

2 kg (4 lb 8 oz) clams
   (vongole)
4 French shallots, peeled
   and thinly sliced
2 celery stalks, thinly sliced
   on a 45-degree angle
1 lemon, sliced as thinly
   as possible
1 tablespoon salt
1 tablespoon raw
   (demerara) sugar
1½ tablespoons vegetable oil
400 ml (14 fl oz) dry cider
2 tablespoons butter
1 large handful mixed beach
   herbs, picked and washed
sourdough, to serve

Use fresh, live clams if possible. Soak them in fresh water to get rid of any sand and draw out some of the salty sea water. Soak for a couple of hours and store in the fridge, covered with a wet towel, until ready to cook.

Place the vegetables and lemon in a bowl with the salt and sugar. Mix really well and leave to marinate for an hour. Drain the vegetables and discard the liquid. Rinse under cold water and squeeze out any extra liquid.

Place a wok or large saucepan over high heat. Add the vegetable oil and throw in the clams. Stir the guys up, then add the cider and marinated vegetables. Place a lid on the wok and leave to cook for 4 minutes. Remove the lid, leaving the wok over high heat, and add the butter and beach herbs. Shake the wok to melt the butter into the sauce. This will thicken the sauce and give the dish a nice, glossy shine. Taste for seasoning – it should be pretty good already, thanks to the salt from the marinated vegetables and natural taste of the clams.

Crack a cider and serve with sourdough to mop up all the sauce.

PORK LOIN, FERMENTED PEAR SAUCE & BRUSSELS SPROUTS

This is a classic combination but brought to the modern kitchen with the use of fermented pears in the sauce.

SERVES 2–3

600 g (1 lb 5 oz) pork loin
8 brussels sprouts
½ teaspoon ground
   aniseed myrtle
olive oil
250 ml (9 fl oz/1 cup)
   dry cider
½ cup Fermented Pears
   including juice (see page 64)
2½ tablespoons butter
Pickled Fennel Flowers (see
   page 59) and Pickled Green
   Coriander Seeds (see page
   60), to garnish

NOTE: *Aniseed myrtle can be replaced with fennel seed powder if not available. The pickled seeds and flowers can all be replaced with toasted and ground versions of same.*

Trim any silver sinew from the pork and set aside for 30 minutes to bring to room temperature before cooking.

Trim the bases of the brussels sprouts and peel off the leaves.

Place a large heavy-based frying pan over high heat. Season the pork generously with salt and the aniseed myrtle. Pour a splash of olive oil into the pan and place the pork loin in to caramelise for about 4 minutes. Turn the pork over and leave it to caramelise for a further 4 minutes. The loin will need about 10 minutes in the pan in total, so keep turning it as it caramelises. I like the loin cooked to about medium. If you have a meat thermometer, you're looking for an internal temperature of about 55°C (130°F).

Take the loin out and leave it to rest. Pour the cider into the pan, bring to the boil and add the sprout leaves. Cook over high heat to keep the cider reducing. After a minute of the leaves cooking, throw in the fermented pears and the butter. Shake the pan so the butter melts through the sauce and thickens it. Once the butter has melted, cook for a further minute, then turn off the heat.

Slice the pork loin into roughly 2 cm (¾ inch) thick slices. Lay them on a plate and pour over the sprout-cider-sauce mixture. Finish with some pickled fennel flowers and some pickled coriander seeds.

CARP TAGINE

When I first started cooking with carp, my peers were very confused. A lot of them thought I was nuts, but there was real motivation to make delicious recipes with the feral fish. European carp is the biggest pest in Australian rivers. They seem to be unstoppable, thriving in almost all conditions and their eggs can travel a bloody long way before the young fish are born.

On the plus side, they're packed with nutrition. On the down side, they don't taste the best. So here's the challenge: what to do with a fast-breeding fish that's in abundance and really good for us, but tastes pretty ordinary.

I found this tagine was my favourite of all the recipes I tried, as the spices help mask the carp's muddy flavour. I've also had decent success making carp croquettes. Have a chat with your fishmonger and source a carp that has been purged of any less-than-desirable water. If you are game, catch the carp yourself and keep it alive in a large tub of fresh water to purge for a few hours before cooking.

SERVES 4

1 large carp, about 1.5 kg (3 lb 5 oz)
6 kipfler (fingerling) potatoes, chopped into 2 cm (¾ inch) pieces
12 pieces of okra
4 coriander (cilantro) roots
2 teaspoons coriander seeds
1 teaspoon ground turmeric
2 teaspoons cumin seeds
60 ml (2 fl oz/¼ cup) olive oil
2 brown onions, finely chopped
4 garlic cloves, finely chopped
2 cm (¾ inch) piece ginger, finely chopped
1 large pinch of saffron
1 medium handful coriander (cilantro) leaves
2 tablespoons honey

Gut, scale and fillet the carp as you would any other fish, or ask your fishmonger to do it for you. Be sure to cut out all the bones. Dice the fillets into roughly 2.5 cm (1 inch) pieces and set aside. Wash the frame well in cold water.

Put the frame in a saucepan with 3 litres (105 fl oz/12 cups) of water, place over high heat and bring to the boil. Once boiling, turn down to a simmer. Skim the foamy impurities from the top as it cooks for 45 minutes. Strain the water and discard the frame. Set aside the stock for later.

Place the potato in a small saucepan and cover with water. Add a large pinch of salt and place over high heat. Bring to the boil, turn down to a simmer and cook until a small knife can be easily pushed through a spud piece.

Cut the okra into 2 cm (¾ inch) pieces and cover with cold water to soak and draw out the sliminess. Soak the coriander roots in cold water to remove any sand and thinly slice.

Toast the spices in a dry frying pan for a few minutes, and then grind to a fine powder using a spice grinder or mortar and pestle.

Place a heavy-based saucepan over high heat. Add the olive oil along with the onion, garlic, ginger and coriander roots. Cook for 6 minutes or until tender and the onion is translucent. Add the toasted ground spices and the saffron. Keep stirring and cook for a further 2 minutes.

Add the stock and bring to the boil. Leave to simmer for 5–10 minutes. Drain the okra and add to the pan. Cook for about 5 minutes. Add the potatoes and the fish, leave to simmer for 8 minutes, then turn off the heat. Add the coriander, honey and a pinch of salt, and stir gently to combine. Taste for seasoning.

Serve on its own or with some lemon couscous or quinoa.

ROAST CHOOK 'BO SSAM'

This is the ultimate 'got no time to cook' dinner. This recipe is inspired by the bo ssam, an Asian shared meal. You can use up any pickles or vegetables that are in your fridge. It's basically whatever you like wrapped in a lettuce leaf with sauce and pickles.

It's a great dish to use up leftover roast meats and other bits lying around. The notion behind this chicken version is to grab a whole roast chook on your way home and have a fresh, healthy meal ready in 10 minutes.

SERVES 3–4

1 roast chicken
2 small lettuces (I like to use baby cos/romaine but any lettuce will do)
1 avocado, sliced
300 g (10½ oz) Kimchi (see page 63)
200 g (7 oz) pickles
2 handfuls bean sprouts, trimmed
150 g (5½ oz) mixed fresh herbs
Hot Sauce (see page 221) and Mayonnaise (see page 216), to serve

Pick and shred the flesh from the chook (keep the frame for broth-making purposes). Place the flesh in a serving bowl. Pick and wash the lettuce leaves. Place the lettuce on a platter and top with the chicken, avocado, a pile of kimchi, pickles, bean sprouts, herbs and sauces on the side.

This dish looks great as it's full of vibrant colours and the part that took the most effort was probably swinging past the shops to pick up a roast chook.

QUAIL, VERJUICE & GRAPES

This dish is inspired by one of my all-time favourite Australian chefs, Maggie Beer. I love her philosophy of accessible, wholesome food and ethical beliefs and practices.

SERVES 3–4

6 butterflied quail
large bunch grapes
125 ml (4 fl oz/½ cup) verjuice
250 ml (9 fl oz/1 cup) Chicken
   Broth (see page 74)
60 g (2¼ oz) butter
2–3 thyme sprigs,
   leaves picked
polenta and green salad,
   to serve

Season the quail with salt. Place a large frying pan over high heat. Once hot, put in half the quail skin side down and leave to caramelise for a few minutes until golden brown. Turn the quail and cook for a minute on its underside. Remove the quail from the pan and repeat with the remaining birds.

Once the second batch of quail is browned and out of the pan, throw the grapes and verjuice in there. Bring to the boil and add the broth. Boil and reduce by half. Throw in the butter and shake the pan to melt it through.

Place all the quails back in and move them around the pan so they all get a healthy coating of sauce. Cook for about 5 minutes at this stage until the birds are just cooked through. Sprinkle with thyme leaves.

Place the quail on a plate and pour over the sauce and grapes. Serve with soft white polenta and a crunchy green salad on the side, a delicious combination.

STEAK, EGGS, FRIED BREAD & CAPSICUMS

This is a simple, single-pan dish that can be cooked for one person or ten. It's also my go-to meal when I get home late and need a filling dinner quickly.

SERVES 1

1 steak, about 200 g (7 oz)
olive oil
1 egg
1 tablespoon butter
120 g (4¼ oz) stale bread,
    roughly torn into 2 cm
    (¾ inch) pieces
60 g (2¼ oz/½ cup) sliced
    roasted red capsicum
    (pepper) or cherry tomatoes
1 tablespoon chopped flat-
    leaf (Italian) parsley
Hot Sauce (see page 221),
    to serve (optional)

NOTE: *I like to use skirt steak for this recipe, but any steak is suitable.*

Put a large frying pan over high heat. Season your steak with salt and dress with a little olive oil. Place the steak in the hot pan and cook for a few minutes until caramelised. Turn the steak and relocate it to one side of the pan.

Crack an egg into the pan and add the butter. Fill any gaps in the pan with the torn-up bread. By this stage your steak should be cooked and the egg ready, making sure the yolk is still runny. Gently slide the egg on top of the steak and remove both of them to rest. The egg will stay warm on top of the steak.

Continue to fry the bread until golden. Turn the heat off and throw in the capsicum and chopped parsley. Toss together and serve alongside the steak and egg.

Drizzle with a little olive oil and finish with cracked pepper. A cheeky splash of hot sauce doesn't go astray either.

Sensible people in Africa, Asia and South America have been eating insects for centuries and have a long history of using these nutrient-rich critters in their cuisine. Insects are excellent sources of protein, fibre, vitamins, minerals and healthy fats.

They are fast growing – only taking a few weeks to reach maturity – and can be bred on waste in extremely compact spaces. For many people around the world, they're an excellent low-maintenance food, and thanks to enthusiastic online suppliers, you can now purchase bugs with minimal fuss.

Sometimes the insect is the star of the dish, deep-fried and sprinkled with a spicy coating or served up on skewers. That's the way they're presented in markets in Bangkok and other parts of Thailand – the perfect crispy snack food to go with a cold beer. They're a must-try treat for adventurous eaters who are willing to give anything a go. But often they're used in a less challenging manner – fermented and made into sauces, ground into flour, blended into drinks or snuck into dishes in all sorts of clever ways.

Insects are the latest Big Thing in the health and fitness industry, enticing gym junkies with the promise of vitamins, minerals and a huge protein hit. Cricket and mealworm flours are particularly popular as they can easily be hidden in shakes or protein bars. When out of sight, they're out of mind. It's easier to consume the little creatures if they're not staring you in the face. Other great hiding places are pancake batters, cakes, biscuits, pizza dough and burgers.

Edible insects are easy to find online. They're sold in dehydrated form, as a crispy deep-fried snack, in flours and powders as a muscle-building protein and as a novelty (chocolate-covered silkworm anyone?). Thailand has a healthy – and growing – local industry, with thousands of insect farms and several enterprising companies that package up their crickets, mealworms, centipedes and waterbugs and ship them to converts around the world.

Bugs are big in the States, with lots of farms growing, harvesting and selling insects to restaurants and health-conscious Americans.

VARIETIES

Crickets are probably the most popular consumable insect. They have a mild taste, so once fried can take on the flavour of whatever salts or spices you add to them. They can be dehydrated and eaten whole, or ground up and added to all sorts of different foods. Mealworms are another favourite. Like crickets, they're an excellent fried, salty snack but can also be ground up and used in baking. Ants are tangy and crunchy, often with a lemony flavour.

SUSTAINABILITY

I believe that insects could play a pivotal role in a sustainable food future. Not only can they provide us with a protein kick, they can also help reduce our food waste. Sad-looking spinach, outer cauliflower leaves or any other organic waste can be recycled as feed for edible bugs, which then become an excellent low-maintenance food source. It's recycling at its best.

Insects can also be grown in incredibly small spaces. When you think about the amount of water and agricultural land required to produce meat or crops, bugs win the prize for the most sustainable, space-efficient protein source there is. And they don't need a fancy location – unused, dead spaces where nothing else can grow can become productive by establishing small-scale insect farms. Plus they only take a few weeks to grow to full size so you can always guarantee a steady supply.

For many of us, the thought of chomping on a crispy cricket challenges our idea of what food is. But the benefits – healthy bodies, low cost and sustainable food production – make insects an obvious choice to help feed the growing population of our planet.

CRISP CRICKETS, MEALWORMS & AUSTRALIAN SEVEN SPICE

I know what you're thinking. 'Bugs? Who are you trying to kid? Worms are for the garden bed, not the dinner plate.' I'm very aware it's not easy to convince people to eat crickets and worms, but a salty, spicy snack like this is a great way to start the process (especially because it goes so well with beer).

SERVES 2

vegetable oil, for deep-frying
50 g (1¾ oz) crickets
30 g (1 oz) mealworms
½ teaspoon Australian Seven
   Spice (see page 211)
Fermented Chilli Paste
   (see page 48) and wild herbs
   (optional), to serve

NOTE: *For a little freshness, finish with whatever wild herbs you can get your hands on. Wood sorrel (oxalis) is great as it adds a zingy sour note.*

The bugs will more than likely be frozen so be sure to take them out of the freezer a couple of hours before cooking. Heat the oil in a deep-fryer or large saucepan to 180°C (350°F). If you don't have a cooking thermometer, throw a cricket in and if it bubbles vigorously, the oil is hot enough. Carefully place the crickets and mealworms into the oil, making sure it doesn't boil over. Stir often and cook for 3–4 minutes until golden and crisp.

Remove from the oil with a slotted spoon and drain well on paper towel. Mix with the spice and season with salt to taste.

Place in a small bowl (a clay tapas bowl is very attractive for this) and add a few random dots of fermented chilli paste and some wild herbs, if using.

Serve straight away with a hard-earned Aussie beer.

WHITEBAIT, ANTS & MYRTLE

Small school fish are very fast breeding so you can feel good about your choice to eat them. The ants are in the dish for flavour, not just because it's fun to serve insects. They have a sour lemon-pepper flavour and work really well with fried seafood. This is kind of like my version of salt and pepper squid (emphasis on 'kind of').

You can buy rice flour from the shops but it's also really simple to make your own. Just blend some uncooked rice on high speed until you have a fine powder. You can pass it through a sieve if it's not super fine. I like to use brown rice as I find it has a better flavour and more fibre.

SERVES 4

2 tablespoons ants
2 tablespoons salt
ice cubes
500 g (1 lb 2 oz) whitebait
45 g (1½ oz/¼ cup) rice flour
30 g (1 oz/¼ cup) cornflour
   (cornstarch)
1 teaspoon ground
   lemon myrtle
2 teaspoons ground
   aniseed myrtle
vegetable oil, for deep-frying
Mayonnaise (see page 216),
   to serve

NOTE: *You can source a variety of edible insects from specialist online shops. If you can't find the myrtle in your local supermarket, you can also buy this online from specialist herb and spice sites.*

A day or so before you want to serve this, combine the ants and salt so the flavours infuse. Leave the ant salt at room temperature for the first day, then store it in the fridge. It will keep for a week, so you can make a larger batch if you like and have it on hand.

Now, I would never normally suggest washing fish but whitebait is an exception. Fill your sink or a large bowl with cold water. Add a few ice cubes to really chill it down. Add a large pinch of salt. Pour in the fish and mix it around with your hands. This will clean any slimy bits away and remove a few of the tiny scales. Drain well and place on paper towel to dry.

Mix the rice flour and cornflour together with the myrtle. If you own a deep-fryer, add vegetable oil and heat it to 180°C (350°F). If not, pour about 2 litres (70 fl oz/8 cups) of vegetable oil into a large saucepan and heat to the same temperature. If you don't have a cooking thermometer, simply place the end of a fish in the oil; if it bubbles and fries straight away, it's ready.

Dust half of the fish in the flour–myrtle mix, making sure the fish is evenly coated all over. Shake off any extra flour and carefully place the fish into the hot oil. Stir often so they cook evenly and don't stick together. Cook for about 3 minutes until light brown and crisp. Scoop 'em out with a slotted spoon and dry on paper towel. Repeat the process with the remaining fish, letting the oil heat up again first.

Once drained on the paper towel, place the fried fish into a bowl and toss with a few large pinches of ant salt. Serve stacked on a plate with a generous amount of mayonnaise and some extra ant salt on the side.

6.
SWEETS

For me, simplicity is the key when it comes to sweets. I've never been a fan of fatty, heavy desserts that require lots of time and tricky techniques. I like the lighter-style dishes that leave you feeling refreshed but not sluggish.

Many of my sweets are fruit-based, but I sometimes like to incorporate veggies in there as well. You may be surprised at the type of ingredients that work well in a sweet dish. Kale granita? Delicious. Not only does it inject a fresh, herbal flavour to the dish, but provides amazing colour on the plate as well.

I love the potential for contrasts that desserts offer – soft and crunchy, hot and cold, sweet and sharp. Try the Barbecued Bananas & Chocolate Ice Cream (see page 185) or the Rhubarb, Sour Cream, Almond Praline & Granita (see page 189), and you'll see what I mean.

Remember that these desserts are all open to adaptation. Feel free to replace ingredients with similar fruits or flavours you have available. You could use apples or pears instead of rhubarb, lemon myrtle or aniseed myrtle instead of lemon verbena, and your favourite nuts instead of almonds. Whatever takes your fancy – or, importantly, whatever you have sitting in the fruit bowl, or in the fridge or pantry. Don't be afraid to experiment. Here's your chance to be creative!

WATERMELON JELLY, MACADAMIA MILK & STRAWBERRIES

I love fruit and jelly. It's one of those classic dessert combinations that works so well. There's the wonderful coolness and appealing textures as well as big flavours that pack a punch. Here, the macadamia milk gives some weight and body to the dessert, playing the same role as cream without the heaviness.

SERVES 6

1 kg (2 lb 4 oz) watermelon, skin removed
3 titanium-strength gelatine sheets or 1½ teaspoons powdered gelatine
iced water
40 ml (1¼ fl oz) lime juice (about 1 large lime), plus finely grated zest
1 tablespoon caster (superfine) sugar
250 g (9 oz) strawberries, hulled and sliced into discs
edible flowers (optional)

MACADAMIA MILK
155 g (5½ oz/1 cup) macadamia nuts
500 ml (17 fl oz/2 cups) milk
1 tablespoon raw honey
1 teaspoon xanthan gum

NOTE: *You'll find gelatine sheets in some supermarkets. If you can't get your hands on them, replace with powdered gelatine and follow the packet directions. Xanthan gum can be found in the health-food section of supermarkets.*

Start by taking 750 g (1 lb 10 oz) of the watermelon and juicing it in a food processor or juicer. Strain the juice through a fine sieve, using some elbow grease to squeeze any remaining juice out of the pulp. The remaining 250 g (9 oz) will be used when you serve the dessert, so store it somewhere out of harm's way.

If using gelatine sheets, soak them in a bowl of iced water for 5–10 minutes until they bloom (hydrate and expand).

Meanwhile, add the lime juice and zest to the watermelon juice and combine. Put 200 ml (7 fl oz) of the juice mixture into a small saucepan and place over medium heat. Add the sugar and stir until dissolved. Once the juice begins to warm (but not boil), add the bloomed gelatine, squeezing out any extra liquid first (or add powdered gelatine here, if using). Stir until dissolved.

Remove from the heat and stir in the remaining juice mixture. Pour into a small container and place in the fridge.

To make the macadamia milk, preheat the oven to 160°C (320°F). Spread the macadamia nuts out on a baking tray and roast in the oven for 8 minutes or until golden. Set the nuts aside to cool, then place the cooled nuts, milk and honey in a food processor. Blend until the milk becomes smooth, then add the xanthan gum and blend until thickened, place in a container and refrigerate. This can be made in advance and will last in the fridge for 3–4 days.

To serve, use a tablespoon to scoop out some jelly and place in a bowl. There's no need to cut these out perfectly; simple blobs will do. Next, scoop out small balls of watermelon flesh and dot around the plate. Pour the macadamia milk around the jelly and place the strawberries on and around the jelly. Sprinkle with some edible flowers, if using, for a decorative touch.

PEAR & ALMOND TART

Here I've used the classic combination of pear and almonds and taken it up a notch with the addition of orange zest and star anise. A great dessert to feed a crowd, it's even better served with your own homemade Yoghurt (see page 41) or a top quality cream.

SERVES 6–8

1 quantity Shortcrust Pastry
    (see page 33)
plain (all-purpose) flour,
    for dusting

PEAR FILLING
200 g (7 oz) sugar
2 cinnamon sticks
3 star anise
2 bay leaves
4 whole cloves
finely grated zest and juice
    of 1 orange
3 beurre bosc pears

ALMOND FRANGIPANE
160 g (5½ oz) butter
165 g (5¾ oz/¾ cup) caster
    (superfine) sugar
1 vanilla bean, split
    lengthways and
    seeds scraped
4 eggs
160 g (5½ oz) almond meal
2 tablespoons freshly
    milled flour

Combine the squares of cold sweet pastry, lightly dust with flour and roll into a round between two sheets of baking paper until about 3–4 mm (⅛–¼ inch) thick. Place on a baking tray and put into the fridge to rest for 1 hour.

Line a 30 cm (12 inch) round tart (flan) spring-form tin with baking paper and then drape the pastry over the lined tin, gently pressing it into the base and trimming off any overlap. Prick the base of the tart shell with a fork a few times and place into the freezer.

To make the pear filling, pour 750 ml (26 fl oz/3 cups) of water into a medium saucepan, add the sugar and spices and place over low heat. Add the orange zest and juice, then simmer for 15 minutes. Remove from the heat and let it cool for 20 minutes.

Peel the pears and place them in the pan, making sure they are completely submerged. Bring the syrup to a very gentle simmer again and keep it simmering for 4–5 minutes. Remove from the heat and let the pears sit in the hot liquid for 15–20 minutes until tender. Remove the pears from the liquid and let them cool.

Place the syrup back on the heat, reduce by two-thirds and reserve for serving.

Preheat your oven to 170°C (340°F).

To make the almond frangipane, use an electric mixer fitted with the paddle attachment to cream the butter until smooth and pale. Add the sugar and vanilla seeds and continue to mix, scraping down the side of the bowl every couple of minutes to make sure it creams evenly. When the butter mixture is creamy and pale, start adding the eggs, one at a time. Don't add the next egg until the previous one is well incorporated. When all the eggs have found their new place in life and the mix is light and fluffy, add the almond meal and flour. Mix for 3–4 minutes to incorporate.

Quarter the pears and remove the cores. To assemble, fill the frozen tart shell to three-quarters full with the frangipane. Arrange the pears on top, keeping a couple of quarters aside for serving.

Place the filled tart into the oven and bake for 30 minutes or until the frangipane is cooked through. You will know it's cooked when it's golden brown and jumps back when gently poked.

Let the tart cool for 10 minutes before removing from the tin.

Brush the top with the syrup to give it a nice gloss. Serve with the reserved pears and syrup. Enjoy unapologetically.

PASSIONFRUIT TARTS

The passionfruit vine is a common sight in backyards across Australia, and it's one of the easiest fruits to grow yourself if you have the space. And when you get a glut of fruit in autumn, you can crank out these meringue-topped tarts. The passionfruit seeds are strained out of the pulp, but they don't get wasted: instead they are dried and ground into a powder to sprinkle on top. The dried seeds will keep for up to 6 months, and the juice can be frozen ready for making these tarts.

MAKES 8

200 g (7 oz) passionfruit pulp
plain (all-purpose) flour,
   for dusting
1 quantity Shortcrust Pastry
   (see page 33)
10 egg yolks
250 g (9 oz) caster
   (superfine) sugar
40 g (1½ oz/⅓ cup) cornflour
   (cornstarch)
150 ml (5 fl oz) lemon juice
2 titanium-strength gelatine
   sheets or 1 teaspoon
   powdered gelatine
iced water
250 g (9 oz) butter, cold
   and cubed

MERINGUE
80 g (2¾ oz) egg whites
165 g (5¾ oz/¾ cup) sugar

NOTE: *You'll find gelatine sheets in some supermarkets. If you can't get your hands on them, replace with powdered gelatine and follow the packet directions.*

The day before you want to serve the tarts, strain the passionfruit pulp through a fine sieve over a bowl. You should get about 150 ml (5 fl oz) of juice; reserve this in a container in the fridge. Spread the seeds in a thin, even layer on a piece of baking paper. Place in a dehydrator set at 55°C (130°F) and leave overnight. If you don't have a dehydrator, place on a baking tray and dry in the oven set on the lowest temperature for 4–6 hours.

The next day, blitz the dried passionfruit seeds into a fine powder and set aside.

Grease eight 8 cm (3¼ inch) stainless steel tart rings and coat with flour. Combine the two squares of cold sweet pastry, lightly dust with flour and roll between two sheets of baking paper until 5 mm (¼ inch) thick. Cut out circles of pastry with a 10 cm (4 inch) ring cutter and line the tart rings. Place in the freezer.

Half-fill a medium-sized saucepan with water and place over medium heat. Place a medium-sized stainless steel bowl over the pan of simmering water to make a double boiler. Place the egg yolks and sugar in the bowl and whisk until pale. Add the cornflour and mix until it has dissolved and is free of lumps. Pour in the reserved passionfruit juice and lemon juice and mix until combined.

If using gelatine sheets, soak them in a bowl of iced water for 5–10 minutes until they bloom (hydrate and expand).

Turn the heat down to low; the water in the double boiler should just be very, very lightly simmering. Continue to cook, stirring the mixture with a spatula so it doesn't stick, until it reaches 83°C (181°F) and keep it at that temperature for 10 minutes, stirring rapidly. If you don't have a sugar thermometer, keep the water rolling at a light simmer and stir until the mixture is thick and glossy and generously coats the spatula. Remove from the heat.

Remove the gelatine from the water, squeeze out any extra liquid and stir into the passionfruit mixture (or add the powdered gelatine at this point, if using). Once the gelatine has dissolved, strain the mixture through a fine sieve into a bowl. Add a third of the butter and whisk until dissolved. Repeat twice more until all the butter has been incorporated. Cover with a piece of baking paper, pressing down so that the paper touches the surface of the curd to prevent a skin forming, and refrigerate until set.

Preheat the oven to 180°C (350°F). Remove the tart shells from the freezer and prick the base of each one with a fork. Line the shells with baking paper and fill with baking beads (or uncooked rice or beans). Bake in the oven for 10 minutes, then remove the baking paper and beads. Return the shells to the oven and cook for a further 7 minutes or until the pastry is golden brown and cooked through. Rest the shells for 5 minutes before removing from the tart rings and placing on a wire rack.

Fill the tart shells three-quarters of the way up with the passionfruit curd and refrigerate while you make the meringue. This short time in the fridge will allow the curd to settle.

To make the meringue topping, place a saucepan of water over low–medium heat and bring to a simmer. Place the egg whites and sugar into a medium-sized stainless steel bowl and place over the saucepan to make a double boiler. Turn the heat down to low. Make sure the water isn't touching the base of the bowl. Whisk the egg whites and sugar and bring the mixture to 55°C (130°F) or, if you don't have a sugar thermometer, heat until the sugar starts to become translucent and is slightly hot to touch.

Turn off the heat and remove the bowl from the pan. It is important to wipe any condensation from the base of the bowl as any water in the mix will prevent it from properly whisking. Whisk the egg whites until they are thick and glossy, and the meringue has cooled to room temperature and will hold its shape.

Remove the filled tarts from the fridge and spoon or pipe the meringue on top of the curd. To turn the top of the meringue into a brûlée, preheat your grill (broiler). Place the tarts on a baking tray and place under the grill until the tops begin to turn golden brown. Alternatively, use a blowtorch if you have one. Sprinkle a pinch of passionfruit powder over the tarts to finish.

PASSIONFRUIT TARTS
(SEE PAGE 178)

WHITE CHOCOLATE MOUSSE, KALE GRANITA & ROSELLA JAM
(SEE PAGE 182)

WHITE CHOCOLATE MOUSSE, KALE GRANITA & ROSELLA JAM

This might sound like a wacky combination, but it's a delight to the senses, with lots of different textures and bold, bright colours and flavours. The icy green granita features kale and cucumber, which gives it a wonderful soothing, herbal quality. When frozen with some sugar, it has an amazing fresh, ripe flavour. Then there's the decadent creaminess of the white chocolate mousse and the tartness of the rosella jam. Sweet, sour and creamy, with a vegetable base, it's an in-your-face dessert that your dinner guests will not forget in a hurry.

SERVES 4

WHITE CHOCOLATE MOUSSE

1½ titanium-strength gelatine sheets or ¾ teaspoon powdered gelatine
iced water
2 tablespoons full-cream (whole) milk
70 g (2½ oz/¼ cup) Yoghurt (see page 41)
130 g (4½ oz) white chocolate
1 egg yolk
60 g (2¼ oz) egg white
2 tablespoons sugar
135 ml (4½ fl oz) thin (pouring) cream

NOTE: *You'll find gelatine sheets in some supermarkets. If you can't get your hands on them, replace with powdered gelatine and follow the packet directions.*

INGREDIENTS CONTINUED OPPOSITE
➡

Start by making the mousse. If using gelatine sheets, soak them in a bowl of iced water for 5–10 minutes until they bloom (hydrate and expand).

Meanwhile, place a half-filled saucepan of water over low–medium heat and bring to a simmer. Sit a stainless bowl on top of the saucepan to create a double boiler. Add the milk and yoghurt and gently heat. Remove the gelatine from the water, squeeze out any extra liquid and add to the milk mixture (or add powdered gelatine at this point, if using) and stir until it has dissolved.

Place the chocolate in a mixing bowl. Pour in the heated milk mixture and stir it as the chocolate starts to melt. Keep stirring and add the egg yolk.

In another bowl, whisk the egg white until it starts to foam. Add the sugar and keep whisking to form a meringue that's thick and glossy. In a third bowl, whisk the cream to soft peaks. Yes, this recipe uses a lot of bowls.

Fold the meringue into the white chocolate mixture, being gentle enough not to knock too much air out, but also mixing enough to disperse the meringue evenly. Fold the cream through next, stopping when it's just incorporated. Pour into a container, cover and refrigerate for a minimum of 4 hours.

Next, make the kale granita. If using gelatine sheets, soak them in a bowl of iced water for 5–10 minutes to bloom (hydrate and expand). Pour 100 ml (3½ fl oz) of the kale juice into a small saucepan and place over low heat. Add the sugar and stir over low heat until it has dissolved. Remove from the heat and, while still warm, add the bloomed gelatine, squeezing out any extra liquid first (or add powdered gelatine here, if using). Stir until it has dissolved and pour the mix into the remaining kale juice. Add the cucumber juice and stir. Pour into a container and freeze.

Once frozen, drag a fork across the ice to form ice crystals. When all of the solid ice block has been turned into crystals, return it to the freezer.

To make the rosella jam, put the rosella flowers, sugar, lemon juice and 100 ml (3½ fl oz) of water in a medium-sized saucepan and place over low–medium heat. Stir occasionally until the sugar has dissolved. Brush down the inside of the saucepan with a wet basting or pastry brush to remove any sugar crystals that may be sticking around. This will stop any caramelising that may happen during the cooking process that could potentially change the flavour of the jam.

Continue to cook over low heat, reducing the liquid to a syrup consistency and cooking the rosella through. This should take about 20–30 minutes.

When the rosella squashes under pressure and there is a glossy shine to the syrup, remove it from the heat. Cool for 5 minutes before placing the mixture in a food processor, then blitz until it's smooth and glossy. Now, let it cool right down.

To serve, spoon 1 tablespoon of rosella jam onto a plate. With a clean spoon, scoop a generous amount of the mousse on top of the jam and cover the mousse in kale granita. Serve immediately.

KALE GRANITA
1 titanium-strength gelatine
    sheet or ½ teaspoon
    powdered gelatine
400 ml (14 fl oz) kale juice
75 g (2¾ oz/⅓ cup) sugar
300 ml (10½ fl oz)
    cucumber juice

NOTE: You'll need an electric juicer so you can make the kale and cucumber juice yourself. About 1 kg (2 lb 4 oz) of kale and 400 g (14 oz) of cucumbers should do the job.

ROSELLA JAM
500 g (1 lb 2 oz) frozen rosella
    (hibiscus) flowers
250 g (9 oz) sugar
juice of 2 lemons

NOTE: Frozen rosella (hibiscus) flowers can be bought online or from gourmet food stores.

BARBECUED BANANAS & CHOCOLATE ICE CREAM

This is an easy way to end a summer barbecue on a high note. The ice cream is simple enough to make if you have an ice-cream machine; however, good quality ice cream can be picked up from the shops to make this dessert even more of a cinch. I really like the contrast of hot and cold here.

SERVES 6

400 ml (14 fl oz) full-cream (whole) milk
400 ml (14 fl oz) thin (pouring) cream
8 egg yolks
150 g (5½ oz) sugar
100 g (3½ oz) chocolate (of your choice)
6 large ripe bananas
100 g (3½ oz/⅓ cup) Almond Praline (see page 189)

NOTE: *If you're serving this dessert to your kids, you might prefer to use a child-friendly milk chocolate, but if you're keen on a richer, more sophisticated flavour, use a 72% cocoa dark chocolate.*

Half-fill a saucepan with water and bring to the boil, then reduce the heat so the water is lightly simmering. Meanwhile, place the milk and cream in another saucepan, bring to the boil and quickly remove from the heat.

Whisk the egg yolks and sugar in a stainless steel bowl until smooth and pale. Keep whisking while you pour over the hot milk mixture until it's well combined.

Place the bowl over the pan of lightly simmering water to create a double boiler. Stir gently with a wooden spoon and bring to 85°C (185°F). If you don't have a sugar thermometer, heat the custard until it's glossy and thick enough to coat the back of the spoon. If you take it any further than this, it will start to curdle. You don't want it to curdle.

Remove the bowl from the heat, add the chocolate and stir until incorporated. Refrigerate for at least 4 hours before churning in an ice-cream machine according to the manufacturer's instructions.

Barbecuing the bananas is a bit of summer fun. Leave them in their skins and whack them straight onto a sizzling hot barbecue. Cook for about 4 minutes on each side until the banana skins are black and tender to the touch.

Serve them straight from the barbie, making a slit down the length of each one and pulling the skin slightly apart to hint at the sweet flesh underneath. Sprinkle the flesh with some almond praline and place on a large plate with the chocolate ice cream in a serving bowl for everyone to share.

LEMON MASCARPONE PARFAIT & FROZEN CUMQUATS

This parfait is a highly adaptable, proven recipe that works really well. I've made it with many different flavours and in many different versions. Any citrus works – passionfruit, orange, mandarin, lime. At times I've ditched the lemon and incorporated almond milk instead, but you can use any nut milk to develop a lovely nutty flavour. A simple milk-based parfait is a great alternative, but you can also add some *dulce de leche* (caramelised condensed milk), which is delicious and a little decadent. Basically you can adapt this dish to suit your tastes and pantry. Once you've made this once, try another flavour and see how it goes!

SERVES 6

8 egg yolks
250 g (9 oz) caster (superfine) sugar
150 ml (5 fl oz) lemon juice
finely grated zest of ½ lemon
500 g (1 lb 2 oz) mascarpone
150 ml (5 fl oz) thickened (whipping) cream
12 cumquats, frozen
ground lemon myrtle, to serve

NOTE: *Most supermarkets stock lemon myrtle these days. Alternatively, you can buy dried myrtle online from herb and spice specialists.*

Place a medium-sized saucepan one-third filled with water over medium heat. Bring to the boil.

Combine the egg yolks, sugar, lemon juice and zest in a stainless steel bowl. Place the bowl over the pan of boiling water to create a double boiler and whisk until the mixture is thick and has quadrupled in size. Remove from the heat and whisk until cool.

Fold in the mascarpone. Whip the cream and fold it in, too. Pour the mixture into a 22 x 12 x 6 cm (8¾ x 4¾ x 2½ inch) terrine mould or loaf (bar) tin and freeze for a minimum of 4 hours or, better yet, overnight.

To serve, fill your kitchen sink with a few centimetres of warm water and bathe the frozen mould to loosen the parfait. Turn onto a serving plate. Grate the frozen cumquats generously over the top and sprinkle with a little lemon myrtle. The parfait can be served as a whole piece to share or cut into thick slices for single servings.

LEMON MASCARPONE PARFAIT
3 FROZEN CUMQUATS

WHEY, LEMON VERBENA 3 GINGER SORBET
(SEE PAGE 188)

WHEY, LEMON VERBENA & GINGER SORBET

Whey is the liquid remaining from straining curdled milk (see page 41), and it gives this sorbet, pictured on the previous page, a lovely silky consistency. The gelatine is optional: it will stabilise the mixture but is not essential to the finished dish. If lemon verbena isn't available, lemongrass can substitute. I'm a big fan of the zing the ginger brings to this party.

SERVES 6

200 g (7 oz) caster (superfine) sugar
12 large lemon verbena leaves, plus extra to garnish (optional)
2 titanium-strength gelatine sheets or 1 teaspoon powdered gelatine (optional)
800 ml (28 fl oz) Whey (see page 41)
2 cm (¾ inch) piece ginger, finely grated

NOTE: *Lemon verbena leaves are often available at farmers' markets or gourmet grocers and food stores. You'll find gelatine sheets in some supermarkets. If you can't get your hands on them, replace with powdered gelatine and follow the packet directions.*

Place 200 ml (7 fl oz) of water and the sugar in a small saucepan and bring to the boil. Throw in the lemon verbena and let the liquid reduce for 5 minutes. Remove from the heat, leave the syrup to cool, then strain out the lemon verbena leaves.

If using gelatine sheets, soak them in iced water for 5–10 minutes until they bloom (hydrate and expand). Remove from the water and squeeze out any extra liquid, then add to the verbena syrup (if using powdered gelatine, add it here). Add the whey and ginger and mix them in, too. If you're not using gelatine, just add the whey and ginger to the verbena syrup and mix.

Churn in an ice-cream machine according to the manufacturer's instructions until firm. Place in the freezer for at least 2 hours to set fully. Serve garnished with extra lemon verbena leaves, if using. (If you don't have an ice-cream machine you can always simply freeze the mixture and turn it into a granita.)

RHUBARB, SOUR CREAM, ALMOND PRALINE & GRANITA

The crunch of the praline, the softness of the tender rhubarb and the crystalline granita make this dessert an experience in taste and texture.

SERVES 4

2½ tablespoons raw (demerara) sugar
1 cinnamon stick
2 aniseed myrtle leaves
1 pepperberry
½ vanilla bean, split lengthways and seeds scraped
finely grated zest and juice of 1 orange
550 g (1 lb 4 oz) rhubarb, rinsed, trimmed and cut into 5 cm (2 inch) lengths
4 heaped tablespoons Sour Cream (see page 38) or crème fraîche, to serve

ALMOND PRALINE
100 g (3½ oz) almonds
150 g (5½ oz) sugar

NOTE: *You may find aniseed myrtle leaves in speciality tea shops or the tea section of gourmet supermarkets. Alternatively, try online herb and spice specialists, where you'll also be able to buy pepperberries.*

Preheat the oven to 170°C (340°F). In a medium saucepan, combine 300 ml (10½ fl oz) of water with the raw sugar, spices, vanilla seeds, orange zest and juice. Bring to the boil and then turn off the heat.

In a deep-sided roasting tin, arrange the rhubarb in a single layer. Pour over the hot liquid and cover the tray with foil. Bake in the oven for 15 minutes.

Remove the tin from the oven and reduce the temperature to 160°C (320°F). Carefully peel off the foil and remove the rhubarb from the liquid, place in a large bowl and let it cool down to room temperature on the kitchen bench, then refrigerate. Strain the cooking liquid into a container and place in the freezer for at least 4–6 hours (but overnight is even better). Once frozen, drag a fork across the ice to form ice crystals. When all of the solid ice block has been turned into crystals, return the granita to the freezer.

Meanwhile, to make the almond praline, line a baking tray with baking paper. Spread the almonds out on the tray and bake for 12 minutes, then set aside.

In a heavy-based saucepan, heat the sugar over low–medium heat. Once all the sugar has dissolved, continue to cook until it's a dark amber colour, but don't let it burn. Remove from the heat and pour the liquid over the almonds, covering every last one. Leave to cool, then break into pieces.

Remove the granita from the freezer just before you're ready to serve. Assembling this dessert is a simple layering exercise. Spoon some sour cream or crème fraîche into a bowl, add a few pieces of poached rhubarb, sprinkle almond praline on the top and add a spoonful of bright red granita.

SOFT-CENTRED CHOCOLATE & WATTLESEED CAKES

There are so many chocolate lovers in this world that it's become the golden rule that every restaurant has chocolate somewhere on the menu ... and the same is certainly true of cookbooks. You don't have to go far down the confectionery aisle of a supermarket to see that coffee and hazelnut flavours are a tried-and-true match with chocolate, but my take on the chocolate cake uses the delicious Australian native ingredient of wattleseed to replicate this traditional combination.

MAKES 4

3 egg yolks
2 whole eggs
55 g (2 oz/¼ cup) sugar
125 g (4½ oz) 72% cocoa dark
   chocolate (or whatever
   chocolate you fancy)
100 g (3½ oz) butter
250 g (9 oz/1⅔ cups) freshly
   milled flour
2 teaspoons wattleseed
mascarpone or sour cream,
   to serve

NOTE: *Wattleseed is now available in some supermarkets but can also be found easily online. It imparts a lovely cacao and hazelnut flavour.*

Grease four metal 7 cm (2¾ inch) cake moulds and line with baking paper. Place on a baking tray.

Using an electric mixer fitted with the whisk attachment, whisk the egg yolks, whole eggs and sugar until light and fluffy and able to hold a figure-eight shape.

Place a medium-sized saucepan one-third filled with water over medium heat. Put the chocolate in a stainless steel bowl and place over the pan of simmering water (to create a double boiler), stirring until melted. Add the butter and stir until melted in with the chocolate, then carefully remove the bowl from the saucepan.

Pour a third of the egg mix into the chocolate mix and fold through. Repeat this twice more, then fold through the flour. Pour the mix into the lined moulds until just below the lip and place in the freezer for a minimum of 4 hours, but overnight's even better.

Once frozen all the way through, heat the oven to 180°C (350°F). Bake the cakes from frozen for 15 minutes. They should rise up and be firm on the sides but soft in the middle.

When cooked, carefully remove the cakes from the moulds and baking paper, and place on serving plates. Scatter with wattleseed and serve with mascarpone or sour cream.

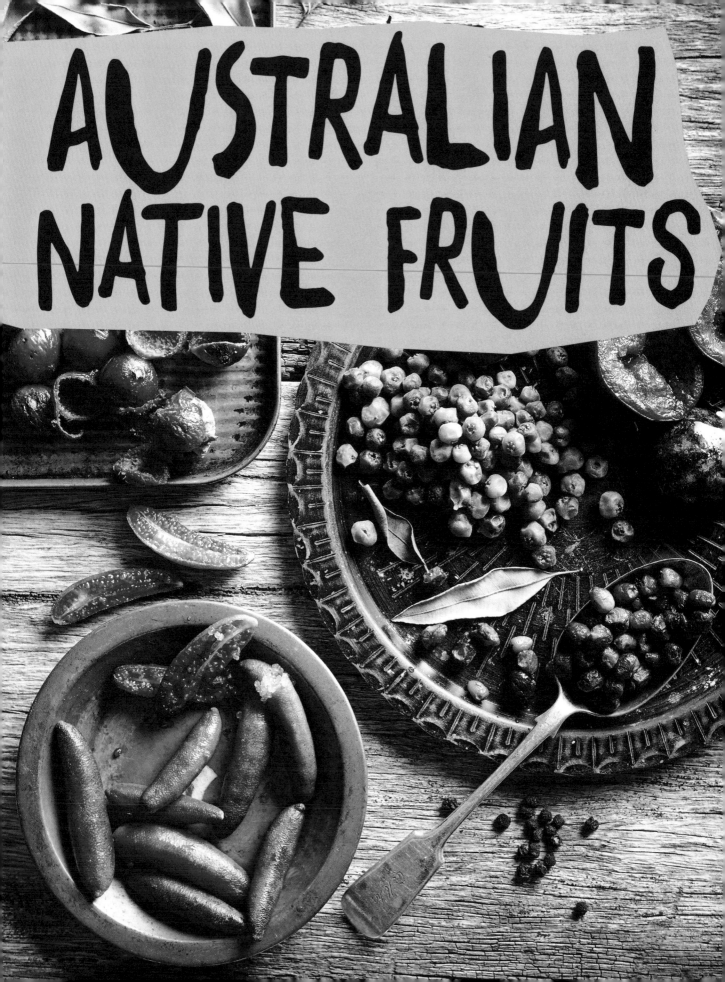

AUSTRALIAN NATIVE FRUITS

Australian native fruits are unique, their flavours and textures as varied and distinct as the ancient continent they come from. They can be used in dishes in all sorts of creative and imaginative ways but seem quite foreign to many of us – even when they're right on our doorstep. Perfectly suited to harsh, arid landscapes, these hardy plants take the prize for sustainability, thriving without the extra water, nutrients and constant care required by many exotics. And they taste delicious!

Despite their remarkable resilience and favoured status in the diets of Indigenous people, these bush foods were largely ignored by Australian chefs for centuries. In the past few decades, though, they have come to the world's attention – first in the tourism-driven 'bush tucker' movement and now in the more recent native produce renaissance.

An important part of defining a country's cuisine is to use the ingredients that grow so naturally and easily in its landscape. Fortunately, native fruits and herbs have finally made their mark on the menus of high-end restaurants and have started making a welcome appearance on supermarket shelves. May they survive and prosper.

NOT A GIMMICK

These amazing ingredients are finally losing the gimmicky 'bush tucker' tag, which can only be a good thing.

The bush tucker label often had negative connotations. Sadly, people came to associate bush tucker restaurants with tacky décor and poorly prepared food while high-end restaurants steered clear. No chef with a talent for matching flavours and developing dishes seriously considered them. It's different today. I guarantee that the top restaurants in Australia will have at least one native ingredient on the menu, and some will have ten or twenty, which is fantastic.

I was first introduced to Australian native fruits when I worked at Star Anise in Perth, but it's really in the last four or five years that I've tried to develop a sense of place with the food I cook. Wherever possible I try to incorporate wonderful native fruits such as riberries, finger limes (citrus caviar), muntries (native cranberries or emu apples), quandongs, rosella (hibiscus) flowers and Davidson plums.

FEAST OF FRUITS

Australian native fruits can introduce a wonderful balancing acidity to meat dishes. They are excellent in jams, pies, tarts and other desserts. Importantly, they're also nutrient-dense and packed with health-giving properties, with high doses of vitamin C found in Kakadu plums and Australian desert limes, and impressive levels of antioxidants in fruits such as quandongs and riberries (almost three times more than in blueberries!).

Australian fruits can be purchased online in frozen or dried form. If you can find these ingredients fresh and in season, that's awesome. They sometimes pop up in gourmet food stores or small supermarkets, or are sold fresh from native fruit stalls at your local farmers' market (depending on where you live). But don't feel bad about having to opt for the frozen or dried version – they're a great alternative to fresh. It's worth remembering that if we don't support native fruits in the way they're available now, they will never get to the point where you can buy them fresh. This very young industry is on a bit of a journey and we can all show our support by trying as many local native fruits as we can.

So make up a batch of delicious lilly pilly jam; pair a Davidson plum sauce with your beef or kangaroo steak; brighten up your seafood dinner with the amazing taste and caviar-like pop of finger lime crystals; and get a welcome boost of antioxidants from a handful of muntries. You won't look back.

7.

DRINKS: TWISTS ON THE CLASSICS

A complementary cocktail can enhance the flavour of a dish, and creating interesting drinks can be a real art. I've had lots of fun working with bar crew through various restaurants making some delicious (and not-so-delicious) cocktails. They don't always work but experimentation is the only way to discover a winning combination.

There are many similarities between the bar and the kitchen, and the same principles apply when it comes to balancing and matching flavours. Seasonal produce and native fruits and spices can all play an important role. In summer you're more inclined to reach for the white spirits, fruits and fresh herbs, while in winter the darker spirits and dried spices work best. Don't be afraid to take a classic drink and turn it on its head with some delicious (and different) local ingredients. It could be the star of the show at your next dinner party.

COCKTAIL EQUIPMENT
Invest in good quality cocktail-making equipment and it will last a lifetime. There's no shortage of cocktail-making sets available online that will have a few of the following items packaged together: a mixing glass, cocktail shaker (Boston shakers are good and can double as a mixing glass in a pinch), jigger/spirit measure, bar spoon (a long-handled spoon with the same capacity as a teaspoon), Hawthorne strainer (a cocktail strainer or sieve), fine strainer, citrus juicer, muddling stick, knife and chopping board.

AUSTRALIAN SPIRITS I RECOMMEND
The Aussie distilling industry has gone gangbusters over the last few years and all signs point to its continuing expansion. These are some of our favourites, but there are plenty more out there. Using native Australian botanicals in the distilling process has opened up new avenues of flavour and has put the local spirits industry on the world map.

VODKA 666 Pure Tasmanian Vodka, Kangaroo Island Spirits, Fire Drum, Hippocampus **GIN** The West Winds, Melbourne Gin Company, Four Pillars, Botanic Australis, Archie Rose, Young Henrys **RUM** Ord River Rum, Far North Queensland Rum Co. **WHISKY** Lark, Bakery Hill, Sullivans Cove, Limeburners, Starward Whisky, Hellyers Road, Nant Distilling Company, Belgrove Distillery **VERMOUTH** Maidenii, Causes & Cures, Regal Rogue **BITTERS** Mister Bitters, Australian Bitters Company.

WILD MULLED CIDER

Mulled cider warms you up on the fiercest of winter nights – the aroma alone is enough to make you forget that it's a single-digit temperature outside. Double or triple the ingredients depending on how many people you have over and how much cider you plan to drink. And, by all means, add a splash of dark spirits such as rum, whisky, calvados or brandy to the final product for extra kick.

SERVES 4

1 litre (35 fl oz/4 cups) scrumpy cider
120 ml (4 fl oz) Spiced Sugar Syrup
   (see page 209)
juice of 1 lemon
slices of lemon and
   cinnamon sticks, to serve

Pour the cider, spiced sugar syrup and lemon juice into a saucepan and bring to the boil, then remove from the heat.

Serve in your favourite mugs and garnish with a slice of lemon or a cinnamon stick or both. Consider your cockles warmed.

BOOZY JUICE

The combination of fresh juice and booze is an age-old tune. You can get tricky and start combining different juices (watermelon and pear, say), but I like to keep it simple by freshly juicing a couple of apples and pouring it over whatever spirits are lying around the house. Whisky, gin, rum and vodka all work well.

SERVES 1

ice
60 ml (2 fl oz/¼ cup) of your favourite spirit
150 ml (5 fl oz) fresh juice

Add some ice to a tall glass and pour in the booze and juice. Drink. Feel refreshed. Repeat.

BOOZY JUICE

SCRUMPY PUNCH

A great one for backyard parties on hot afternoons. We use a flagon or growler for this recipe, but you could use any large jug in the cupboard. If you can find a good Australian cidery (such as Custard and Co.) that sells scrumpy by the flagon, then all the better.

SERVES 4–6

2 litres (70 fl oz/8 cups)
   scrumpy cider
1 lemon
1 orange
1 pink grapefruit
300 ml (10½ fl oz)
   sweet vermouth
1 handful mint leaves
1 Lebanese (short) cucumber,
   sliced lengthways into
   thin pieces
6 strawberries, sliced
1 cinnamon stick
ice

Pour 400 ml (14 fl oz) of the cider into a glass to enjoy while you work. Cut a thick slice from each of the citrus fruits and set aside. Squeeze three-quarters of the lemon, half the orange and a quarter of the grapefruit into a cup. You should have about 100 ml (3½ fl oz) of juice. Pour into the flagon with the remaining cider.

Add the vermouth, citrus slices, about 8 mint leaves, 2 of the long thin slices of cucumber, the sliced strawberries and the cinnamon stick. Secure the lid tightly, turn the flagon upside down and swirl it around to blend the ingredients.

Your punch is now ready to serve. However, I suggest leaving it in the fridge for at least a few hours to allow the ingredients to properly infuse.

Pour over ice in a tall glass and garnish with mint and whatever leftover fruit you fancy.

Consume the punch within 1 week of preparation.

NATIVE FRUITS WHISKY SOUR

The eternally classic cocktail meets the flavours of the bush.

SERVES 1

ice
60 ml (2 fl oz/¼ cup) malt whisky
30 ml (1 fl oz) lemon juice
20 ml (½ fl oz) egg white
1 heaped bar spoon (or teaspoon) of native
   fruit jam such as rosella or Lilly Pilly Jam
   (see page 228)
15 ml (½ fl oz) Spiced Sugar Syrup
   (see page 209)
5 drops of Mister Bitters fig and cinnamon bitters
2 quandongs, halved

Fill a glass with ice and let it stand. Put all the remaining ingredients except the quandongs in a shaker. Seal and shake without ice (this is known as a 'dry shake') for 15 seconds to emulsify the egg white with the other ingredients. Fill the shaker with ice and shake vigorously for another 15 seconds.

Discard the ice from the glass and replace with fresh ice. Single-strain the liquid into the glass using a Hawthorne strainer, place the quandongs on top and serve.

APRICOT BREAKFAST MARTINI

Despite the name, this cocktail is perhaps better suited to Saturday brunch than Monday before work.

SERVES 1

ice
60 ml (2 fl oz/¼ cup) gin
30 ml (1 fl oz) lemon juice
2 bar spoons (or teaspoons) apricot jam
10 ml (2 teaspoons) Basic Sugar Syrup
   (see page 209)
4 small dried rose petals, optional (see page 94)

Fill a martini glass with ice and let it stand. Put the gin, lemon juice, jam and sugar syrup in a shaker, and fill to the top with ice. Seal and shake vigorously for about 15 seconds.

Discard the ice from the martini glass. Pull apart your shaker and double-strain the liquid into the glass using your Hawthorne and fine strainers. Float the dried rose petals on top, if using, and enjoy.

NATIVE FRUITS WHISKY SOUR

APRICOT BREAKFAST MARTINI

LEMON MYRTLE MARTINI

AUSSIE SOUTH SIDE

LEMON MYRTLE MARTINI

James Bond would likely turn his nose up at this version of a martini, but that would be his loss. I love it.

SERVES 1

ice
4 large fresh lemon myrtle leaves
60 ml (2 fl oz/¼ cup) gin or vodka
10 ml (2 teaspoons) dry vermouth

Fill a serving glass with ice and let it stand. Put ice in your mixing glass, give it a quick stir to chill things down, then discard the ice. Scrunch 3 of the lemon myrtle leaves in your hand and place them in the mixing glass, then pour in the booze. Mix and double-strain into the serving glass using your Hawthorne and fine strainers. Serve with a lemon myrtle leaf on top.

NOTE: *For the fresh lemon myrtle leaves, you'll need to grow your own tree – or beg, borrow or steal the leaves from a neighbour or a friend.*

AUSSIE SOUTH SIDE

A refreshing taste of Australia for a spring afternoon.

SERVES 1

ice
60 ml (2 fl oz/¼ cup) white spirit
   (gin, vodka or white rum)
30 ml (1 fl oz) freshly squeezed lime juice
10 ml (2 teaspoons) Basic Sugar Syrup
   (see page 209)
7 Australian river mint (or regular mint) leaves
small plate of ants and 1 lime wedge (optional)

Fill a serving glass with ice and let it stand. Put the spirit, lime juice and sugar syrup, and all but one of the mint leaves, into a shaker, giving the mint a clap between your hands to excite its flavour before throwing it in. Fill the shaker to the top with ice, seal and shake vigorously for around 15 seconds.

Discard the ice from the serving glass. If using ants, rub a wedge of lime around the rim of the glass. Gently press the rim onto your ants, twisting the glass so they stick all the way around the circumference.

Put 3–4 cubes of fresh ice in the glass. Double-strain the liquid from the shaker into the glass using your Hawthorne and fine strainers. Stick the reserved mint leaf on top and serve.

NOTE: *There are specialist online shops where you can buy ants and other edible insects.*

ANISEED MYRTLE & FENNEL POLLEN SAZERAC

The perfect way to begin a night – or end one.

SERVES 1

ice
4 large dried aniseed myrtle leaves
60 ml (2 fl oz/¼ cup) whisky
1 bar spoon (or teaspoon) Basic Sugar Syrup
  (see page 209)
4 dashes of Peychaud's Bitters
small piece of lemon zest, pith removed
fennel pollen, to garnish

Fill a serving glass with ice and let it stand. Put ice in a mixing glass, stir quickly to chill and discard the ice.

Crush the aniseed myrtle leaves in your hands and drop into the mixing glass. Add the whisky, sugar syrup and bitters, fill the glass with ice and stir for 30–40 seconds.

Discard the ice from the serving glass. Double-strain the liquid with your Hawthorne and fine strainers into the serving glass. Squeeze the piece of lemon zest over the glass to release its oils. Sprinkle a pinch of fennel pollen on the underside of the lemon zest, carefully float it on top of the drink and serve.

NATIVE SPICED BLOODY MARY

For a fresh kick, you can also add finely chopped veggies such as tomato, cucumber, celery and chilli. Hangover be gone!

SERVES 1

ice
3 dried bush tomatoes
60 ml (2 fl oz/¼ cup) vodka
15 ml (½ fl oz) lemon juice
6 dashes of Worcestershire sauce
5 dashes of Tabasco sauce (or other hot sauce)
2 large pinches of ground pepperberry,
  plus extra to garnish
2 large pinches of Australian Seven Spice
  (see page 211), plus extra to garnish
1 pinch of pink salt, plus extra to garnish
125 ml (4 fl oz/½ cup) tomato juice
celery stalk or cucumber slice, to garnish

Fill a serving glass with ice and let it stand. Muddle the bush tomatoes, and any other vegetables you feel like, in your cocktail shaker. Add all the other ingredients except the garnishes to the shaker and fill with ice. Slowly 'roll' your shaker end over end to mix and chill the ingredients without frothing things. Taste-test with a straw and add additional Tabasco if you'd like it spicier.

Discard the ice from the serving glass and replace with fresh ice. Single-strain the liquid into the serving glass. Add the celery stalk or cucumber slice and finish with a pinch of salt, pepperberry and Australian seven spice.

NOTE: *Online bush food specialists offer a variety of Aussie fruits, herbs and spices, including bush tomatoes and pepperberries.*

ANISEED MYRTLE & FENNEL POLLEN SAZERAC

NATIVE SPICED BLOODY MARY

BASIC SUGAR SYRUP

Sugar syrup is to cocktails what flour is to baking, and it's a top idea to always have some in the fridge.

MAKES ABOUT 700 ML (24 FL OZ)

500 ml (17 fl oz/2 cups) water
500 g (1 lb 2 oz) raw (demerara) sugar

Pour the water into a medium saucepan and bring to a low boil. Add the sugar and stir until it has dissolved. Pour into a bottle, seal and store in the fridge for up to 6 months for future imbibing.

SPICED SUGAR SYRUP

This delicious syrup has many uses – not just for cocktails, but also for poaching fruit and making mulled wine or cider.

MAKES ABOUT 700 ML (24 FL OZ)

500 ml (17 fl oz/2 cups) water
500 g (1 lb 2 oz) raw (demerara) sugar
2 cinnamon sticks
2 star anise
8 whole cloves
15 fennel seeds
8 cardamom pods
10 juniper berries
zest of 1 large orange
zest of 1 large lemon
¼ vanilla bean, split lengthways
  and seeds scraped

NATIVE INGREDIENTS (OPTIONAL)
large pinch of dried lemon myrtle leaf
large pinch of dried cinnamon myrtle leaf
large pinch of dried aniseed myrtle leaf

Pour the water into a medium saucepan and bring to a low boil. Add the sugar and as many of the listed spices as you like or have in the pantry. If you don't have any fennel seeds, for example, it's not the end of the world. Leave it to simmer for 10 minutes; your kitchen will smell like Christmas.

Remove from the heat and let it cool. For best results, store in the fridge overnight with the spices left in, then strain before using. This syrup will keep in a sealed bottle in the fridge for up to 6 months.

NOTE: *Most supermarkets stock lemon myrtle these days. You should be able to track down the other myrtle varieties from online herb and spice specialists.*

SPICE MIXES

My cupboard is packed with spice mixes that I use on everything from burgers and bugs to beef ribs. Stored in airtight containers, these will last a good few months, after which time they'll start to lose their flavour.

MANGROVE
TEENAGE NINJA
MYRTLE

7½ SPICE

LEMON MYRTLE
LEAF GROUND

UEL POLLEN

BUSH

SPICE

AUSTRALIAN SEVEN SPICE

This is my version of Chinese five spice and it's perfect on barbecued meats, vegetables and fried bugs. If you don't feel like eating bugs with your beer then perhaps try it rubbed into barbecued chicken wings or slow-cooked beef ribs. The individual spices can vary due to season, availability and personal taste, so think of this as a rough guide. Use double the amount of mountain pepper if you like your spice mixes hot.

1 tablespoon ground bush tomato
1 tablespoon ground lemon myrtle
1 tablespoon ground wattleseed
1 tablespoon ground pepper leaf
1½ tablespoons ground mountain pepperberries
2 teaspoons ground aniseed myrtle
1 tablespoon ground mangrove myrtle

NOTE: *While most of the Australian ingredients used in this book can be substituted with something non-native, this is the one recipe I urge you to stick to (otherwise it will become 'mostly Australian seven spice').*

Mix all ingredients. Store in an airtight container or jar.

MIXED PEPPER

Pepper is very big in flavour and for that reason I treat it more as a spice than a seasoning. This mouth-numbing mix is great for giving zing to red meat and vegetables. It also works well lightly sprinkled over big-flavoured pan-fried fish.

2 tablespoons whole mountain pepperberries
2 tablespoons whole sichuan peppercorns
1 tablespoon ground pepper leaf

Toast the mountain pepperberries and sichuan peppercorns in a dry frying pan over medium heat until nice and fragrant. Leave to cool and then mix in the pepper leaf. Grind to a powder and store in an airtight container or jar.

ZA'ATAR

As well as being an excellent seasoning for grilled breads, this Middle Eastern spice mix is also perfect for jazzing up roasted vegetables and grain salads.

2 tablespoons sesame seeds
1 tablespoon dried thyme
2 tablespoons dried oregano
1 tablespoon sumac

Toast the seeds in a dry frying pan over medium heat until they just start to turn golden. Turn off the heat and add the other spices, giving the pan a toss – the residual warmth will be enough to bring them to life. Let them cool and store in an airtight container or jar.

BAHARAT

This very fragrant spice mix is great on roasted vegetables, oily fish and all meats. It can also be mixed into mayo. I use a mild, unsmoked paprika but you can use the sweet smoky variety if you prefer.

8 whole cloves
4 star anise
2 tablespoons black peppercorns
1 tablespoon cumin seeds
2 tablespoons coriander seeds
3 tablespoons paprika

Put all the spices except the paprika in a dry frying pan. Place over medium heat and toast the spices for a few minutes until fragrant, tossing them often. Remove from the heat and leave to cool. Once the pan is cool enough to touch, mix in the paprika.

Grind what is now a very heady-smelling mix into a fine powder using a mortar and pestle or spice grinder. Store in an airtight container or jar. Use liberally.

NOTE: *You can buy some of these Australian native ingredients in everyday supermarkets, but all can be easily found online from bush food or herb and spice specialists.*

8.

DRESSINGS, SAUCES & SPREADS

A homemade sauce or dressing using fresh, good quality ingredients tastes better than anything you can buy at the supermarket – and will be a lot cheaper, too.

These recipes are easy to master and will make the difference between a good-tasting meal and a great-tasting one. All you need is a pantry stocked with some fundamentals: vegetable oil, apple cider vinegar, good-quality olive oil, garlic, lemons, spices and herbs.

I like to have a supply of these dressings, sauces and spreads in the fridge or pantry and often use them to quickly turn a few leftovers or sad-looking ingredients into something special. Pair a simple roast chook from the shop with some of the aioli or hot sauce in a baguette and you've got a delicious dinner. Retrieve the chunk of cabbage from the back of the veggie crisper, add some fresh herbs and the spiced lemon dressing and you've got a great side salad. And having a homemade jam or nut and chocolate spread at the ready means you've always got afternoon snacks covered.

Most of these condiments keep for a while, too, so you'll have them on hand to spoon on or pour over any meal, any time.

MAYONNAISE

The only thing that beats a good homemade mayo is a sandwich made with homemade mayo. I encourage you to double this recipe – it will easily last in the fridge for a week and it's great to use not only on sandwiches, but in salads and on the side of meat and veg dishes. It can quickly be flavoured with spices or you can add capers, chopped cornichons, herbs and lemon to make a simple tartare sauce.

MAKES 250 G (9 OZ)

4 egg yolks
1 tablespoon dijon mustard
1 tablespoon apple
  cider vinegar
250 ml (9 fl oz/1 cup)
  vegetable oil

NOTE: *Turning your homemade mayo into homemade aioli is a cinch. Finely dice the rind from 1 preserved lemon and finely chop 2 garlic cloves, then add to the mayo at the same time as the mustard and vinegar.*

Twist up a tea towel (dish towel) and place in a circle on the bench. Place a mixing bowl in the middle of the towel. (The tea towel should help keep the bowl from moving around too much while you whisk away with one hand.)

Put the egg yolks, mustard and vinegar into the bowl and whisk together. Slowly pour the oil into the mixture while whisking as fast as possible (use a jug if you have one – it needs to be a slow stream of oil flowing in, and pouring from a jug is an easy way to control it). If the oil is added too quickly, it won't be incorporated and will split from the eggs. It sounds a bit tricky, but just take your time and everything will be fine.

Once all the oil is whisked in, add some salt to taste. Store in a jar in the fridge. It will last up to 2 weeks.

Spread. Enjoy. Be merry.

SMOKED TOMATO
KETCHUP
(SEE PAGE 218)

MAYONNAISE

SMOKED TOMATO KETCHUP

I love to have this sauce on hand. Like any good tomato sauce, it's awesome on a burger, chips or a meat pie as well as being a great condiment to jazz up eggs on toast. Use this any time you would usually reach for the store-bought tomato sauce.

I use paperbark to smoke the tomatoes as it burns very quickly and smokes a lot. It's also easy to find in suburban streets and parks. You can use fine smoking chips or sawdust if you can't get your hands on any.

THERE WILL BE SMOKE. Put your exhaust on high and open the windows so you don't set off the fire alarm. The smoking can also be done outside on a barbecue, which probably isn't the worst idea if you want to avoid your house smelling like a bushfire.

Very important safety tip: be careful when lighting the paperbark and make sure there's nothing near the stove that could also catch fire.

Also important to note: this is a lot of fun.

MAKES ABOUT 2 LITRES (70 FL OZ/8 CUPS)

2 kg (4 lb 8 oz) tomatoes, halved lengthways
1 tablespoon salt
2 teaspoons Mixed Pepper (see page 211)
2 dry paperbark sheets
1½ tablespoons olive oil
1 large brown onion, finely chopped
2 garlic cloves, finely chopped
2 red chillies, deseeded and thinly sliced
250 ml (9 fl oz/1 cup) balsamic or red wine vinegar
50 g (1¾ oz) raw (demerara) sugar

Combine the tomatoes in a bowl with the salt and mixed pepper. Leave to sit for 30 minutes. This will draw out excess liquid.

While the tomatoes are doing their thing, it's time to set up the 'smoker'. Line a heavy-based roasting tin with foil. Shred the paperbark into small strips, enough to cover the surface of the tin. Place over high heat and leave for about 10 minutes so it gets really hot.

Place the tomatoes on a wire rack that fits inside the roasting tin. Position a few metal moulds (or anything metal and sturdy) in the tray that will later be used to prop up the tomatoes and stop them from touching the bark.

The bark may well set alight without further encouragement thanks to the heat from the tray, but if not, use a match to get a small fire started.

The bark will flame and burn out very quickly. Once the flame has died, quickly place the tray of tomatoes on the moulds and cover with a lid or more foil. Leave the heat on high for a further 5 minutes. Don't be tempted to remove the lid or foil to check how things are going as all that amazing smoke will escape.

Turn off the heat and leave for 15 minutes. Remove the lid or foil. Peel the skins off the tomatoes and give them a gentle squeeze to remove any extra liquid and some of the seeds. Roughly chop and set aside.

Place a heavy-based saucepan over medium heat, then add the olive oil and the chopped onion. Stir often. When the onion starts to colour lightly after 3–4 minutes, add the garlic and chilli. Cook for a further 3 minutes. Add the chopped tomatoes and cook for 5 minutes, stirring often. Next, add the vinegar and sugar and cook for a further 15 minutes.

Pour the tomato mixture into a blender and purée until smooth while slowly pouring in 185 ml (6 fl oz/¾ cup) of water. Check for seasoning as it may need some more salt and mixed pepper.

I like to store this tomato sauce in a squeeze bottle in the fridge for easy use. Give a bottle to family or friends – there's plenty to share around. It will keep for about 2 weeks.

NAM JIM DRESSING

It's fresh, zesty and healthy, and great with papaya salad, rare beef, pork and all kinds of seafood. You can't make a Thai beef salad without it and it also makes an excellent dipping sauce for fish cakes.

MAKES ABOUT 125 ML (4 FL OZ/½ CUP)

2 coriander (cilantro) roots, with about
   10 cm (4 inches) of the stems attached
3 large red chillies, deseeded and finely chopped
2 teaspoons raw (demerara) sugar
1 garlic clove
3 tablespoons lime juice
1½ tablespoons fish sauce

Soak the coriander roots and stems in cold water for 10 minutes to make sure there's no dirt left in the roots. Drain well and roughly chop.

Using a mortar and pestle, pound the chilli and sugar for a few minutes until the chilli breaks down and starts bleeding juice. Add the coriander and garlic and pound for another 2 minutes until a wet paste forms. Add the lime juice and fish sauce. Mix and taste for seasoning. If it's too hot for your taste, add some more sugar. Additionally, if the limes are really sour you might need to add another dash of fish sauce. The aim is to find a balance to your taste of sweet, sour, salty and hot.

This dressing will keep for a few days but is best used immediately as the lime juice will dull in flavour the longer it's out of the lime.

SPICED LEMON DRESSING

This dressing takes seconds to make and packs an amazing wallop of flavour. It's an easy way to spruce up a green bean salad for Sunday lunch, add flavour to haloumi or even lightly dress beef carpaccio.

MAKES ABOUT 230 ML (7¾ FL OZ)

4 tablespoons lemon juice
150 ml (5 fl oz) olive oil
1 tablespoon raw honey
2 large pinches of ground cinnamon
1 large pinch of allspice

Put all the ingredients into a small jar. Shake it really well and presto! You're done. Any leftover dressing will keep in the fridge for up to 1 week.

NASTURTIUM SAUCE

Nasturtium leaves have a beautifully crisp, peppery flavour and deserve to be treated as far more than just a garnish. This sauce is perfect with fish but also works wonderfully with shellfish and roasted vegetables. I use it in a sea mullet dish (see page 148) but you might also like to mix a little through seafood pasta with clams (vongoles) and mussels or as a dipping sauce with salt and pepper squid.

MAKES ABOUT 300 G (10½ OZ)

4 egg yolks
1 tablespoon mustard
1 tablespoon lemon juice
1 garlic clove, coarsely chopped
1 green chilli, deseeded and coarsely chopped
½ teaspoon dried mountain pepper leaf
250 ml (9 fl oz/1 cup) vegetable oil
100 g (3½ oz) nasturtium leaves, well washed

Place the egg yolks, mustard, lemon juice, garlic, chilli and pepper leaf into the blender (a jug-style blender is best to make this sauce, but a food processor can also be used). Blend on a medium speed and slowly start pouring in the oil. Once about a third of the oil has been added, throw in the nasturtium leaves. Continue blending and adding the rest of the oil.

Season with salt to taste. The sauce should be bright green, thick and full of life. It will last for about 1 week in the fridge.

NOTE: *You can easily source dried mountain pepper leaf from online herb and spice specialists. For the nasturtium leaves, you'll need to grow your own or beg, borrow or steal some from neighbours or friends.*

HOT SAUCE

My version of Sriracha sauce only has a few ingredients, but the depth of flavour comes from the fermenting of the chilli. Use it as you would Sriracha – that is on a lot of things and particularly leftover pork-belly sandwiches.

MAKES ABOUT 350 ML (12 FL OZ)

1 cup Fermented Chilli Paste (see page 48)
1 large garlic clove
2 tablespoons honey
125 ml (4 fl oz/½ cup) vegetable oil

Place the chilli paste, garlic and honey in a jug-style blender. Start the blender and gradually increase the speed. Slowly pour in the oil, season to taste with salt and you're good.

This sauce will keep for weeks in the fridge. If it sits dormant for a while, the ingredients might start to separate a bit – just give it a good shake and it will come back to life.

I usually store it in a squeeze bottle for convenient use because it's bloody addictive.

SPICED LEMON DRESSING
(SEE PAGE 220)

HOT SAUCE
(SEE PAGE 221)

NASTURTIUM SAUCE
(SEE PAGE 221)

NAM JIM DRESSING
(SEE PAGE 220)

ALMOND & BUTTERMILK
DRESSING

TAHINI YOGHURT

ALMOND & BUTTERMILK DRESSING

All you need to know is that this dressing plus cos (romaine) lettuce equals success. Chop the most cheerful cos lettuce you can find into quarters, arrange on a plate and spoon over the dressing. If you wanted to be really fancy, you could scatter a tablespoon or three of crisp, diced pancetta over the lettuce, too.

MAKES ABOUT 250 ML (9 FL OZ/1 CUP)

4 tablespoons almond meal
125 ml (4 fl oz/½ cup) buttermilk
85 g (3 oz/⅓ cup) Sour Cream (see page 38)
2 tablespoons lemon juice
zest of ½ lemon

Toast the almond meal in a frying pan over medium heat until lightly golden and then leave to cool. Place all the ingredients in a bowl and mix well. Put the spoon down because that's all you need to do.

This will last for a few days in the fridge but is best used straight away.

TAHINI YOGHURT

This take minutes to make and livens up the simplest of meals. I like it best on roasted vegetables but it's also delicious with lamb. Try it slapped on a lamb burger with bright, fresh tomato slices, or use it to go with Chickpea Falafels (see page 104) or dolloped on barbecued chook wings with a sprinkle of Za'atar (see page 211).

MAKES ABOUT 330 G (11½ OZ)

260 g (9¼ oz/1 cup) Yoghurt (see page 41)
1 garlic clove
1 lemon
4 tablespoons tahini

Place the yoghurt in a mixing bowl. Microplane in the garlic clove and the zest of the whole lemon. Add the tahini and the juice from half the lemon. Mix well and season with salt and pepper.

Store the tahini yoghurt in an airtight container in the fridge. It will last about 4–5 days.

HOT & SOUR DRESSING

This is a super simple dressing with a huge kick, and it's perfect with chicken, beef, kangaroo and shellfish.

For a really quick meal, make this dressing and while it's cooling, grab a good quality roast chook from the shops, shred the chicken meat into small pieces and mix in a salad bowl with crunchy leaves, cucumber, tomato and onion. Pour over the cooled dressing and you're done!

Feel free to tweak the sugar and chilli levels here to suit your personal taste.

MAKES ABOUT 250 ML (9 FL OZ/1 CUP)

2 tablespoons Fermented Chilli Paste (see page 48)
120 ml (4 fl oz) lime juice
2 tablespoons apple cider vinegar, ideally with a live 'mother' (see page 49)
3 tablespoons caster (superfine) sugar
1 tablespoon salt

Combine all the ingredients in a small saucepan with 2 tablespoons of water. Bring to the boil, then remove from the heat and leave to cool. This dressing will keep for a few days but is best made on the day it's going to be used.

SAFFRON DRESSING

This is a beaut dressing for a seafood salad (squid is particularly good) or mixed with brown rice topped with crunchy vegetables. A light summer salad with saffron dressing, a glass of rosé and good company is an excellent way to spend an afternoon.

MAKES ABOUT 320 ML (11 FL OZ)

6 thyme sprigs, leaves picked
2 French shallots, finely chopped
1 garlic clove, finely chopped
2 large red chillies, deseeded and finely chopped
1 tablespoon honey
60 ml (2 fl oz/¼ cup) apple cider vinegar, ideally with a live 'mother' (see page 49)
pinch of saffron
250 ml (9 fl oz/1 cup) olive oil

In a mixing bowl, combine the thyme, shallots, garlic, chilli, honey, vinegar and saffron. Leave to sit on the bench for about 30 minutes to marinate. The vinegar will cure and mellow all the ingredients. Whisk in the olive oil and season with salt and pepper.

This dressing is always better the next day after it's made, and will keep for up to 1 week in the fridge.

SAFFRON DRESSING

HOT 3 SOUR DRESSING

LILLY PILLY JAM

When I was a kid I remember lilly pilly trees all over the neighbourhood. For some reason we knew them as Chinese apples. I remember eating them but not being a fan – their raw taste is pretty full on for a kid.

I now cook with lilly pillies whenever I can. They're perfect in rich sauces for red meats and delicious in desserts. They don't fruit for very long but when they do, oh man, do they fruit. I always preserve some for later use. They freeze well, but I like to make this jam, too. It's awesome on toast, in cakes and in gin-based cocktails.

MAKES ABOUT 600 G

1 kg (2 lb 4 oz) lilly pilly berries
4 apples
about 750 g (1 lb 10 oz) raw (demerara) sugar (the exact amount will depend on the amount of fruit mixture)
juice of 1 lemon

Wash and remove any stems and leaves from the berries. Peel and roughly chop the apples into 2 cm (¾ inch) chunks, leaving the core in. The skins of the apples can be dried in a low-temperature oven to be used later on in cakes or desserts if you like.

Place the berries and apples in a large heavy-based saucepan. Add water to the level of the fruit. Bring to the boil, then reduce the heat and simmer for 30 minutes. The berries should be cooked to the point that the flesh has separated from the seeds. Pass everything through a sieve, pressing all the flesh through and only leaving the seeds.

Measure the fruit mixture in a jug and remember the amount. Clean the pan and return the fruit mixture to it.

Add an equal amount of raw sugar to the pan as there is fruit mixture – so if there is 750 ml (26 fl oz/3 cups) of fruit mixture, add 750 g (1 lb 10 oz) of raw sugar. Also, add the lemon juice. Place over high heat and stir to dissolve the sugar. When it's just about to boil, lower the heat to a simmer and cook for 30 minutes.

Test the consistency of the jam by spooning a small amount of it onto a small plate and placing it in the freezer for 5 minutes. Once cold, run your finger through the jam. If it's thick, that means the jam is ready to go.

Turn off the heat and let it sit for a further 30 minutes. Stir again, then pour into sterilised jars. Put the lids on straight away and gift one of the jars to someone special. The jam will keep for at least 6 months in the fridge.

SANDALWOOD NUT & CHOCOLATE SPREAD

I like to think my Aussie version of the famous chocolate hazelnut spread is a world first, but there may be a grandmother in a small town somewhere who has been making something similar for 75 years – stranger things have happened. Instead of hazelnuts, I use sandalwood nuts, which are native to Western Australia and a by-product of the sandalwood industry. They have a popcorny, nutty taste with this crazy gummy texture and they are also packed with protein.

MAKES ABOUT 350 G (12 OZ)

200 g (7 oz) sandalwood nuts
150 g (5½ oz) 72% cocoa
    dark chocolate
3 teaspoons coconut oil
¼ teaspoon pepperberries
1 teaspoon wattleseed
1 tablespoon honey
1½ teaspoons salt flakes

NOTE: Sandalwood nuts can be found online without too much hassle. If they're not available, substitute with macadamia nuts. Many supermarkets stock wattleseed these days, but you can easily buy it online from bush food or herb and spice specialists, and they'll also offer pepperberries.

Preheat the oven to 160°C (320°F).

Place a medium saucepan one-third filled with water over medium heat. Bring to a light simmer.

Meanwhile, spread the sandalwood nuts on a baking tray and place in the oven, toasting for 18 minutes or until golden brown.

While the nuts are toasting, put the chocolate and the coconut oil in a stainless steel bowl and place over the pan of simmering water to create a double boiler. Stir occasionally until the chocolate has melted, then remove from the heat.

Put the chocolate, toasted nuts and remaining ingredients in a food processor and blend to form a smooth paste. Store in a sterilised jar. This keeps for up to 2 months in the fridge.

QUALITY

LILLY PILLY JAM
(SEE PAGE 228)

SANDALWOOD NUT 3
CHOCOLATE SPREAD
(SEE PAGE 229)

PEANUT BUTTER

PEANUT BUTTER

Try this rich, delicious homemade spread on your banana pancakes in the morning. It's a great start to the day. Excellent on toast with the Lilly Pilly Jam (see page 228) or just by itself, this flavoursome spread can also add a touch of sweet nuttiness to cakes and biscuits. It's difficult to source locally grown organic peanuts, but it's worth trying to track them down if you can.

MAKES ABOUT 280 G (10 OZ)

265 g (9½ oz) peanuts
2 teaspoons caster
   (superfine) sugar
2 teaspoons salt
1 teaspoon grapeseed oil

Preheat the oven to 160°C (320°F).

Spread the peanuts on a baking tray and bake for 12 minutes or until golden brown. While the peanuts are still hot, put them in a food processor and begin to blend on a medium–high speed.

Add the sugar and salt. You will notice the nuts will turn into something that looks like breadcrumbs. Continue to blend until the natural oils are released and it begins to look like a paste. At this point, slowly add the grapeseed oil. Continue to blend until smooth and homogenised.

Store in a sterilised jar; it will last for up to 6 months. If the oil splits and rises to the top of the jar, just mix it in again before use.

iNDEX

ACKNOWLEDGEMENTS

There are so many people I need to thank for making this book possible.

Firstly, my parents Mandy and Peter. Thank you for being there through the highs and lows over the past twelve years that I've been cooking. Your constant support and encouragement has got me to where I am today.

Jo, my amazing girlfriend. When I was buggered from working too much and just wanted to watch the cricket and have a beer, Jo quietly let me know that I should be doing some writing or recipe testing. If it wasn't for Jo, I never would have got this book finished. Jo also assisted me through the recipe testing and had a big hand in the dessert and freshly rolled and milled sections.

Terry Durack and Jill Dupleix – it took you a while to convince me to do a cookbook, but I'm so glad you did. Thank you.

Jane Morrow, Virginia Birch and the team at Murdoch. Thank you for having the faith in me to actually write this book and for believing in my cooking. Madeleine Kane and Sarah Odgers made the book look amazing. Susie Ashworth and Callan Boys helped turn my poor grammar and writing into beautiful words. Mark Roper and Lee Blaylock, the styling and photographs are epic.

Joost, thank you for constantly inspiring me! You have shaped me into the cook I am today with your enthusiasm towards ethical farming and food.

Caleb Baker, cheers mate. Caleb and I had a great night or two making the cocktails!!!

Tony and Ilana, thank you for letting me shoot the book at Oakridge. It works out that a barrel room makes a great studio.

Lastly, thank you to all the cooks who I've been lucky enough to work with.

Published in 2016 by Murdoch Books, an imprint of Allen & Unwin

Murdoch Books Australia
83 Alexander Street
Crows Nest NSW 2065
Phone: +61 (0) 2 8425 0100
Fax: +61 (0) 2 9906 2218
murdochbooks.com.au
info@murdochbooks.com.au

Murdoch Books UK
Ormond House
26–27 Boswell Street
London WC1N 3JZ
Phone: +44 (0) 20 8785 5995
murdochbooks.co.uk
info@murdochbooks.co.uk

For Corporate Orders & Custom Publishing, contact our Business Development Team
at salesenquiries@murdochbooks.com.au.

Publishing Consultants: Jill Dupleix and Terry Durack
Publisher: Jane Morrow
Editorial Manager: Virginia Birch
Design Manager: Madeleine Kane
Editing and additional writing: Susie Ashworth
Designer: Sarah Odgers
Photographer: Mark Roper
Stylist: Lee Blaylock
Production Manager: Alexandra Gonzalez

A cataloguing-in-publication entry is available from the catalogue of the
National Library of Australia at nla.gov.au.

ISBN 978 1 74336 590 8 Australia
ISBN 978 1 74336 591 5 UK

A catalogue record for this book is available from the British Library.

Colour reproduction by Splitting Image Colour Studio Pty Ltd, Clayton, Victoria
Printed by 1010 Printing International Limited, China

IMPORTANT: Those who might be at risk from the effects of salmonella poisoning (the elderly, pregnant
women, young children and those suffering from immune deficiency diseases) should consult their doctor
with any concerns about eating raw eggs.

OVEN GUIDE: You may find cooking times vary depending on the oven you are using. For fan-forced ovens,
as a general rule, set the oven temperature to 20°C (35°F) lower than indicated in the recipe.

MEASURES GUIDE: We have used 20 ml (4 teaspoon) tablespoon measures. If you are using a 15 ml
(3 teaspoon) tablespoon add an extra teaspoon of the ingredient for each tablespoon specified.